SUCCESSFUL FREELANCING
(HOW TO ENJOY BEING
YOUR OWN BOSS)

SUCCESSFUL FREELANCING
(HOW TO ENJOY BEING YOUR OWN BOSS)

Carolyn D. Smith

ALETHEIA
Publications

Smith, Carolyn D.
Successful Freelancing (How to Enjoy Being Your Own Boss)

Copyright © 2000 by Carolyn D. Smith

Library of Congress Catalog Card Number: 99-97214
ISBN: 1-929129-02-5

Cover design: Gary Rogers
Interior design and composition: Guy J. Smith
Cartoons: Napier Dunn

Aletheia Publications, Inc.
46 Bell Hollow Rd.
Putnam Valley, NY 10579

Printed in Canada

10 9 8 7 6 5 4 3 2 1

CONTENTS

Preface

I have been freelancing as an editor/writer on and off for about three decades. Throughout most of that time I have had an ambivalent attitude toward freelancing. I have chafed at the inability to control work flow or cash flow, complained about the lack of employee benefits like health insurance, and suffered from isolation and feelings of low self-worth. Periodically I have taken full-time, in-house jobs in order to obtain the benefits and enjoy the companionship of co-workers. Yet after a few years I have been inexorably drawn back to freelancing. Why?

It's the freedom.

Consider this: I don't have to set an alarm. I don't have to slog through rain, sleet, or summer heat to commute to work. I don't have to wear expensive and uncomfortable business attire. I don't have to be at a certain place at a certain time. I don't have to sit through endless meetings. And I don't have to endure the stress of office politics. I'm free!

But wait a minute. What about the drawbacks—the income fluctuations, the lack of benefits, the isolation? These are no longer major problems. Over the years I've found ways to deal with them. It has been a long-drawn-out process, full of trial and error. It has been discouraging at times, but gradually I've learned how to manage my freelance life effectively and keep the problems to a minimum. I now find freelancing enriching and satisfying.

In conversations with others who have tried the freelance life, I've found that some people have more difficulty adjusting to freelancing than others do. Some end up back at an in-house job while others become happy, committed freelancers. The difference lies not only in personality and talent but also—and especially—in knowledge and awareness. Those who know what to expect, who gather information and plan carefully before going freelance, have a greater chance of success.

I believe that there are ways to make a freelance career successful from the start, without the trial-and-error process I went through. My goal in this book is to paint a picture of the freelance lifestyle—both the good and the bad—and point out areas where a little knowledge and awareness can prevent the kinds of difficulties that drive many people away from self-employment. This is not a book about running a freelance business; there are plenty of books available that deal with the business aspects of freelancing (see the Appendix). While those books cover such topics as finding clients, keeping records, billing, and controlling cash flow, *Successful Freelancing* focuses on nonbusiness aspects of freelancing such as maintaining self-discipline and coping with feelings of isolation.

If you are deciding whether to "take the plunge" and leave a 9-to-5 job, you will benefit from knowing the kinds of decisions and arrangements you will need to make as a freelancer. If you are already working at home, you will be able to compare your experiences with those of other freelancers and perhaps find ways of making the freelance lifestyle even more satisfying. In either case, I hope you find this book helpful.

Carolyn Smith

Acknowledgments

Many friends, relatives, and colleagues have contributed to this book. For their encouragement, suggestions, comments, and permission to quote their words of wisdom, I am indebted to Leslie Bernstein, Sheila Buff, Gina Doggett, Tony Doggett, Elizabeth Hurley, Laurie Lewis, Elliot Linzer, Ellen Marsh, George Milite, Elsa Peterson, Mary Ratcliffe, Trumbull Rogers, Harriet Serenkin, Guy Smith, and Louise Weiss. May they all live long and prosper!

1
Why Freelance?

THIS IS AN EXCITING time to be freelancing. The continuing revolution in communications technology has combined with corporate downsizing to make freelancing more attractive than ever. More and more people are working for themselves, and loving it.

Perhaps the most salient characteristic of freelancing is the ability to work anywhere you like—at home, in an office, out in the country; wearing pajamas, casual clothing, or perhaps nothing. A few freelancers work at clients' offices, but the majority work at home, either in an office that may be a separate room or a partitioned-off section of a room, or in a room that also serves another function, such as a dining room. There they surround themselves with the tools of their trade (computer, supplies, phone and fax, files), augmented by such essentials as a back-saver chair, a basic reference library, and (very often) something to eat or drink.

Just what kind of creature is this charmed being, the happy freelancer?

What was once a "free lance" is now known as a freelancer. Over the course of centuries, the free lance—a wandering knight who would serve any lord who agreed to support him—has been transformed into the freelancer: a self-employed businessperson who provides valuable services to a number of different employers or clients. While the term *freelancer* is most frequently used in referring to writers and artists, it can be applied to anyone who sells his or her services to employers without a long-term commitment. Thus, editors, proofreaders, translators, designers, photo researchers, desktop publishers, cartographers, caterers, actors, accountants, computer programmers, telemarketers, and hundreds of other kinds of self-employed professionals are freelancers. Sometimes called *knowledge workers* or *consultants,* these self-employed individuals all have one thing in common: They are independent contractors who provide services to more than one client.

Defining the Independent Contractor

What exactly is an independent contractor? This is not an easy question to answer. Because companies sometimes attempt to avoid paying employee taxes (Social Security, unemployment insurance, etc.) by hiring freelancers to work on-site, the Internal Revenue Service has established a set of criteria for use in determining whether an individual is an employee or an independent contractor. Table 1 presents those criteria in the form of twenty questions. If the answer to all or most of the questions is "yes," the individual is classified as an employee.

Of the questions in the table, the most important are those near the end of the list. An independent contractor regularly makes his or her services available to the general public and does not work exclusively for a single company. A relationship with a particular employer can be terminated without liability on either side. And, as many of the questions imply, the main difference between an employee and an independent contractor is the degree of control the person has over the job: The employee must work on the employer's premises and during specific times determined by the employer, while the independent contractor can work wherever and whenever he or she chooses.

The reason this distinction is important has to do with taxes: An independent contractor can deduct all business expenses, including a home office, on a separate tax form. The home office (or the portion of a room used as an office) must be used exclusively for work. Not everyone has enough extra space for a home office, but most people can set aside a few square feet. Having done so, and having found a client or two, they are in business. And as one tax attorney has pointed out, "The best tax shelter in the U.S. is a business of your own."[1] (Note that while most freelancers work at home, this is not a defining characteristic of freelancers. The key characteristic is that the freelancer is not affiliated with any one organization.[2])

In this book I talk mainly about freelancing as it is done by editors, writers, and other people without tangible products who work for more than one client. The clients may be book publishers, magazines, corporations, nonprofit organizations, or any number of other types of organizations. But independent contractors work in many other fields as well, and their

---

1. Seymour S. Kane, CPA, quoted in Marcia Savin, "Former IRS Auditor Gives Us Tax Tips," *The Freelancer*, March–April 1996, p. 1.

2. This also distinguishes freelancing from the increasingly common phenomenon of telecommuting, in which an employee of a company or other organization works at home part of the time but still receives a fixed salary and benefits.

Table 1

Criteria for Determining Employee Status

1. Is the worker required to comply with instructions about when, where, and how the work is to be done?

2. Is the worker provided training that would enable him or her to perform a job in a particular method or manner?

3. Are the services provided by the worker an integral part of the business's operations?

4. Must the services be rendered personally?

5. Does the business hire, supervise, or pay assistants to help the worker on the job?

6. Is there a continuing relationship between the worker and the person for whom services are performed?

7. Does the recipient of the services set the work schedules?

8. Is the worker required to devote full time to the person he or she performs services for?

9. Is the work performed at the place of business of the company, or at specific places designated by the company?

10. Does the recipient of the services direct the sequence in which the work must be done?

numbers are growing as companies merge and downsize, often laying off employees with valuable skills. At the same time, advances in technology—particularly communications technology—are making it easier for employers to hire independent contractors for tasks that formerly would have been done in-house. These factors combine to make freelancing an attractive option for many people. And regardless of their profession, those freelancers will face many of the issues described here— as well as enjoying many of the benefits.

11. Are regular oral or written reports required to be submitted by the worker?

12. Is the method of payment hourly, weekly, or monthly as opposed to commission or by the job?

13. Are business and/or traveling expenses reimbursed?

14. Does the company furnish tools and materials used by the worker?

15. Has the worker failed to invest in equipment or facilities used to provide the services?

16. Does the arrangement put the person in the position of realizing either a loss or a profit on the work?

17. Does the worker perform services exclusively for the company rather than working for a number of companies at the same time?

18. Does the worker in fact not make his or her services regularly available to the general public?

19. Is the worker subject to dismissal for reasons other than nonperformance of contract specifications?

20. Can the worker terminate the relationship without incurring a liability for failure to complete a job?

Freelancing is a business, and there are a number of books that focus on the business aspects of freelancing.[3] But freelancing is also a lifestyle, and when done well it can be extremely satisfying. But it is not for everyone. This book explores the freelance lifestyle, focusing on aspects of freelancing that

---

3. Several of these are listed in the Appendix. See especially *Editorial Freelancing: A Practical Guide*, by Trumbull Rogers.

make it enjoyable while also examining the obstacles and hazards that the freelancer needs to overcome—and can easily overcome with a little knowledge and care.

The Freelance Personality

The decision to start a freelance business involves more than setting up an office and finding clients. As just mentioned, freelancing is a lifestyle as well as a way of making a living. As such, it is closely tied to personality. Just as some people are better suited to sales work than others and some are more technologically oriented than others, there are some people for whom freelancing is a natural extension of the personality and others who would be uncomfortable working outside the familiar office environment.

Central to the freelance personality are feelings about authority and structure versus self-determination and flexibility. To put it in the simplest terms, the desire to be one's own boss is a strong motivator for freelancers. Closely linked to this, of course, is the desire *not* to be bossed by anyone else. I began freelancing after a series of jobs in which I gradually became aware that I disliked having anyone tell me what to do. I also felt constrained by the structure of office work— especially the requirement that I show up at 9 A.M. every day. I wanted to decide when, where, and how I would do my job, and at what pace. I wanted to escape from rules and procedures that I considered arbitrary. In short, I sought *flexibility,* the very core of freelancing.

Freelancers, by and large, are independent, self-reliant, often creative individuals. They have confidence in themselves. They adapt readily to new situations and in fact prefer variety over sameness. They also enjoy working by themselves and have a considerable amount of self-discipline. While there's no point in exchanging one slavedriver for another, if you're looking for an undisciplined, self-indulgent lifestyle and have bills to pay, freelancing is not the answer.

Another key aspect of the freelance personality is a *project,* as opposed to *process,* orientation. Freelancing is done one project at a time. You get a project from a client, you do the work, you turn it in. If you do it well, you'll get another project from the same client. Meanwhile you may be doing other jobs for other clients. There may be times when you don't have any projects at all (a sign that you need to do some marketing—or take a vacation). This is quite different from the typical office job, which may include specific projects but usually involves a steady stream of general, non-project-related work.

Related to the flexibility and fluidity of freelancing is a characteristic that some may see as negative and others as liberating: Freelance work is unpredictable and changeable. The freelancer's workload fluctuates according to the needs of clients. In the case of college textbooks, for example, the need for copyeditors and proofreaders is greatest in the spring, when most books are put into production with the goal of being published before the end of the year. The need for indexers comes somewhat later, when the books have been typeset. Freelancers need to be aware of the cyclical or seasonal aspects of their chosen profession and find other work to fill in the gaps.

There is one more aspect of the freelance personality that deserves emphasis: Freelancing is not for procrastinators. Certainly freelancers are human and have the same tendencies as other normal humans, but if they let the urge to procrastinate get out of control, they will miss deadlines and lose clients. So if you are good at motivating yourself to meet deadlines, you are well suited to freelancing. If not, find another line of work.

Advantages of Freelancing

Just before starting this section I lay down and took a short nap. That's just one of the advantages of freelancing: If you get drowsy in midafternoon, as I often do, you can stop work for a while—something that is a bit difficult to pull off in an office. Freelancers control their work hours, which means that they can work—or not work—whenever they wish. They do not have a fixed work schedule unless they establish one for themselves.

The flexibility of freelancing makes it a useful way to combine work with other desired pursuits, such as birdwatching or volunteer work. It also opens up unlimited possibilities in terms of timing. Trips to zoos, museums, and the like can be planned for midweek, when there are fewer crowds. Vacations can be timed to coincide with periods of low workload; in fact, many freelancers find that they take more vacation time than office workers who are limited to two or three weeks of vacation. In short, freelancing allows you to integrate your work with the rest of your life in creative and fulfilling ways. You don't have to organize your life around the 9-to-5 workday.

Freelancing can also be a viable alternative to an office job when one wishes to stay home with young children. (Note, however, that this requires some care and planning, as discussed in Chapter 3.) For individuals who are physically disabled, freelancing provides opportunities that might not otherwise be available. A freelancer who suffers from rheumatoid arthritis reports that "freelance copyediting and proofreading is the first profession I have had that the arthritis does not interfere with. My clients do not even know about it— I don't take on more work than I can handle and I always meet my deadlines. Freelance editorial work has been the ideal profession for me—physically and mentally."

The freelance lifestyle has many other advantages besides these. An important one is the lack of a commute to and from work. At the end of my workday I can simply walk the few feet to my living room and listen to music; I don't have to face the hassles of crowds, subways, commuter trains, delays, and all the rest. Related to this is greater efficiency: Not having to commute can add two or three hours to the amount of time available for work—or play.

Freelancing also offers the advantage of freedom from office politics and the associated stress. As an independent contractor, the freelancer does not usually face competition for promotions, raises, bonuses, a window office, and all the other trappings of in-house jobs. Nor is the freelancer usually subject to the power games that are endemic to office life. (I say "usually" because freelancing is not entirely free from politics. One always has to be careful in one's relationships with clients, whose personalities and work styles may differ greatly from one's own. There are also certain situations in which the freelancer is a member of a team put together to carry out a specific project. Other members of the team may have conflicting goals regarding such matters as schedule, profits, and quality.)

Some may consider the freelance life frighteningly insecure compared to a regular job, with its fixed hours and steady stream of work—and paychecks. On the surface, this concern seems justified: Freelancers cannot always control the amount of work they have at any given time, and they may occasionally go through "dry spells" when they have no work at all. But these situations are temporary. The freelancer has not been fired, and a little self-promotion usually leads to new projects and an end to the dry spell. Meanwhile the freelancer's in-house counterparts may be biting their nails as mergers are announced and office staffs downsized. When will the pink slip arrive? What will I do if I lose my job? For today's employer, workers are a disposable commodity. From this perspective, freelancing is actually *more* secure than a regular job. Besides, even workers who manage to hold on to their jobs are finding that their real wages aren't increasing. Why not go freelance and gain some control over your economic situation?

Perhaps the best thing about freelancing, though, is that it allows you to express your personality. Rather than fitting yourself to an existing job description, you can design your own job. Provided that you have the necessary skills, you can decide what kinds of professional or "knowledge" work you want to do, what kinds of clients to seek out, and the physical environment in which you will work. If you have skills that are in demand, you can take on only projects that are attractive to you. You can accept only projects that you feel comfortable with, or you can seek out new challenges. Your personality will also be reflected in your hours of work (are you a night owl? an early riser?) and your work habits (more on this in the next two chapters). In short, you will be your own boss in every way.

Some Drawbacks

Of course, freelancing does have some drawbacks. The primary problem with freelancing, mentioned earlier, is unpredictability and the resulting income fluctuations, which sometimes give freelancers the feeling that they are not in full control of their work life. Feast-or-famine situations are not uncommon, and even freelancers with relatively steady workloads sometimes experience dry spells while at other times they find themselves working extremely long hours. There are ways to compensate for these fluctuations (see Chapter 9)—not the least of which is a spouse with a regular job—but if you need to be absolutely certain of your income three or six months from now, freelancing is not for you.

A second drawback of freelancing is the lack of a community of co-workers who are available to help solve problems or just to socialize. Most freelancers work alone; for some, isolation can be a major problem (see Chapter 7). In addition to isolation, there's the fact that responsibility cannot be assigned to someone higher or lower in the hierarchy—the buck stops at the freelancer's desk.

There's also the fact that some people don't consider freelancing a "real job." Be prepared for some raised eyebrows and quizzical looks when you announce that you're going freelance. In fact, freelancers themselves often have an ambivalent attitude toward their lifestyle. I certainly did—and kept going back to in-house jobs as a result. It is only recently that I have become convinced that the advantages of freelancing definitely outweigh the drawbacks.

Not the least of the factors to be considered in becoming a freelancer is the potential cost. Freelancers do not receive employee benefits. They pay the full Social Security tax (referred to as self-employment tax), while employees pay only half. No one pays for their health and life insurance; they must purchase their own. These costs can make freelancing prohibitively expensive if there is insufficient income to cover them along with all the other costs of doing business—equipment, supplies, postage, and so on. Moreover, freelancers do not qualify for worker's compensation, sick days, holidays and vacations, Social Security tax, and other benefits, which together are equivalent to about one-third of a typical employee's income. On the other hand, there are numerous costs associated with office jobs, including clothing, dry cleaning, commuting costs, and lunches. While freelancers do eat and do wear clothes, the costs of these items are much lower when the clothing is jeans or sweats and the lunches are eaten at home rather than in restaurants.

It can also be difficult to get started as a freelancer, unless you either are very lucky or have an alternative source of income. See Chapter 10 for more on the process of going freelance.

* * *

Despite its disadvantages, freelancing has a strong appeal for large—and growing—numbers of people. If you have been thinking seriously about going freelance, there's never been a better time than now. Innovations ranging from Fed Ex to electronic file transfer make it easy to work at home. (I recently moved from New York City to a place in the country with hardly a blip in my work life.) And you won't be alone. According to official statistics, there are more than 10 million self-employed workers in the U.S. labor force, and their ranks are growing as companies continue to merge and downsize.[4] (And when workers are laid off, more work tends to be contracted out to freelancers!) There are also millions of people who freelance in addition to a full-time job. Many people start

---

4. U.S. Bureau of the Census, *Statistical Abstract of the United States: 1999* (118th ed.). Washington, DC: U.S. Government Printing Office, 1999. The largest proportion of independent contractors—over 4 million—are employed in service-related work, but managerial and professional specialties account for over 3 million.

freelancing after retiring from another job, and many others take early retirement to freelance. All of these people—whether they are full- or part-time freelancers—find that they are much happier working for themselves. Why not join them and enjoy the advantages of being your own boss?

2
Getting Comfortable

S OCRATES WAS FAMOUS FOR, among other things, his dictum
"Know thyself." This dictum applies to freelancing just
as it does to many other areas of life. Before embarking
on a freelance career, consider what kind of person you are,
how you like to spend your time, what makes you feel comfortable. Are you a morning person or a night owl? Do you like to
work in one place or move around during the course of the

day? Are you easily distracted? When and where are you at
your most productive? your most creative? These considerations
will form the basis of your work arrangements.

Your Workspace

Since you will be spending much of your time in your workspace,
it's important to make it as comfortable as possible without sacri-
ficing efficiency. You'll need to decide whether to devote part of
your house or apartment to an office or rent space somewhere else.
(Some freelancers like to work in a rented office within walking
distance of home. This helps them structure their workday and
keep all business-related costs separate from personal costs.) I think
it's best not to work in the same room where you eat or sleep,
unless this is unavoidable. It creates an environment that may not
allow you to do your best and in which you may never feel free
from the pressure of work. "Even if I don't have a current assignment," comments one freelancer, "I feel like I can't relax, because
the computer is always there. It's hard to ignore it and just listen
to music or read a book."

As mentioned in Chapter 1, if you decide to use a room
or part of a room at home, the space should be devoted entirely to work. This is essential if the cost of that space (a
percentage of rent or mortgage payments) is to be deducted as
a business expense.

Many freelancers do not do all their work in one place.
Instead, they may move around the house or apartment, working in different rooms, or on a porch or deck, as the spirit
moves them. One occasionally works in bed, another in a rock-
ing chair. Still another works either at her dining room table
or at her computer, which is in the basement. The two loca-
tions have different advantages—the dining room table is in
good light and near the refrigerator, while in the basement
there is no way to see how nice it is outside and, hence, no
temptation to take the day off.

Sometimes there are benefits in working at another location for part of the day—for example, at the library or in the

park. It offers a change of scene and a chance to get some fresh air. Some freelancers work outside whenever possible—under a tree in the park in the spring and fall, or on the beach in summer. Others occasionally work at the library for a change of pace—a few do most of their work there. One freelancer works at a coffee shop from time to time, saying that he likes to be around people sometimes and loves the free coffee refills. (But note that clients do not like to get work with coffee stains on it!) Another says that he doesn't like to work at home because there are too many distractions there.

Some freelancers work in decidedly unusual settings. One writer completed a project on her laptop computer in a hotel lobby, serenaded by cocktail music. But perhaps the most original freelance workplace is an office in a large sailboat, equipped with a notebook computer with built-in fax modem, a cellular phone, and necessary supplies; the owner has called corporate clients from five miles off the coast of Nova Scotia and written press releases while sailing to Maine.

Some freelancers combine work at home with a part-time job or on-site freelancing. "I enjoy getting dressed up and out of the house and seeing another world and faces, as I've worked alone at home so much," is a typical comment.

Expressing Yourself

Now that you have a home office that is all yours, you have an opportunity to express yourself while making your work environment as congenial as possible. Arrange your space to suit your personal needs. Play the kinds of music you like at the volume you prefer. Take full advantage of the fact that you control your workspace.

One of the greatest advantages of a home office, apart from the freedom from commuting and office politics, is that freelancers control their own space and can decorate it in any way that makes them feel comfortable. (Sure, Dilbert can decorate his cubicle, too, but it's not the same.) The pictures and objects in a freelancer's office (or visible from it) make a definite difference in his or her ability to function well at work. One freelancer comments that she needs "a certain sense of beauty—my favorite picture, my cup of tea, a grey sweater and purple scarf, sometimes a beret to keep my brain warm." Another revels in her view of a flowerbed and hummingbird feeder. A third says, "I have three scarves tied to my work chair—black lace, blue velvet, yellow handkerchief." Hardly the environment of the typical nine-to-fiver.

Also important to the freelancer are the comforts of home: quiet and privacy; comfortable furniture;[1] access to the refrigerator, microwave, or hotplate; the presence of plants, flowers, or pets; good lighting, often including natural light (freelancers don't have to wait their turn for a window office); music if desired; "personal totems" such as a special coffee mug; and the freedom to wear whatever clothing one chooses (if any). Typical work outfits of freelancers include bathrobe and slippers; long, loose gowns; jeans; stretch pants; flannel shirts, and sweats (with matching socks, in one case). One writer tends to wear the same articles of clothing every day while working on a particular project—"I have decided it is ritualistic, and it must work, because I always finish the manuscripts."

The freelancer's imagination may play a role in creating the right work environment. One freelancer keeps an album of pictures taken where she has worked—among flowers in a garden, at parks, in the waiting rooms of an endodontist and a car repair shop, and so on. She has labeled it "My Office."

Setting Standards

Like many things in life, the freedom of self-expression that characterizes the freelance lifestyle can be a double-edged sword. But this freedom can be taken to extremes. One freelancer told me that he used to work naked in the summertime. He was so

---

1. A friend points out that office furnishings such as lamps and work surfaces may be less expensive at stores like Home Depot or the local hardware store than at office supply stores.

blasé about this that he did not even bother to throw something on when he answered the door to receive packages. While this attitude could lead to some awkward encounters, the real issue goes beyond clothing or the lack of it. It has to do with setting standards for yourself.

Because no one is watching them, freelancers may become very casual about how and when they work, to the point where they no longer feel like "normal" productive workers. This can have adverse effects on the quality of the work done. I believe that it is important for freelancers to establish some kind of routine that leads into an actual workday (e.g., breakfast, shower, dress, walk the dog, get to work). The details of the routine don't matter; what matters is that the freelancer acts and feels like a real worker running a real business. Freelancing should not be treated as a hobby or pastime. (Although there may be some exceptions, most people can't make money that way.)

Closely related to the need to set standards is the need to maintain self-esteem as a professional with valuable skills, knowledge, and experience. This can be tricky, especially when the flow of work slows to a trickle and the freelancer is home alone with nothing to do. When you work for yourself, you do not have the status that comes from a job title, a specific place in the corporate hierarchy, a window office, and so forth. You have to create these, or their equivalents, for yourself. Your success in this will be reflected in the quality of your work and in your relationships with clients. If you lounge around the house in your pajamas for most of the day and work only when you feel like it, you will not feel like a "real" businessperson; your self-esteem—and the quality of your work—will suffer; and your clients will turn elsewhere for freelance help.

Hours of Work

Because they are free to work whenever they choose, the hours during which freelancers work are, to put it mildly, highly variable. For example:

- 1 P.M. to 6 P.M., Sunday through Friday
- Anywhere between 10 A.M. and 10 P.M., Sunday through Friday
- Never before 10 A.M.
- Monday to Friday, 9 to 5, sometimes 7–11 P.M. as well
- Monday to Friday, except Tuesday; a total of 20 hours
- All day most days
- 7:30 A.M. to 11 P.M.—sometimes forget lunch
- Evenings after an in-house job
- Any time

One new freelancer sums up the situation succinctly: "There are no normal days, alas." On a more positive note, many value the flexibility of their working hours and cite it as a reason for choosing to freelance.[2] A few try to avoid working on weekends, but they are the exception, not the rule. (I have found that I cannot bring myself to stop working for two whole days, with all the lost income that entails.)

Working on weekends, very early in the morning, or late at night is, for some, conducive to concentrated work without interruptions. Also, a night owl can do a job so that the client will receive it in the morning, giving the freelancer an advantage when it comes to small jobs that clients might not otherwise assign to a freelancer.

Elliot Linzer, an indexer who has freelanced for more than twenty-five years, says that he has always been a night owl. While in high school he used to listen to the radio deep into the night, and in college he wrote papers at night. As a freelancer he has maintained the habit of working through most of the night and sleeping from 4 A.M. to noon. Since he hates to be interrupted by phone calls, this schedule has advantages for him (although he is sometimes awakened by calls during the morning, which he answers while half asleep). To

---

2. Some kinds of freelancing are not so flexible. If your business is heavily dependent on telephone communication, you have to be available when clients and vendors are.

drown out street noise, which can be very distracting, he plays a recording of ocean waves. The result, he says, is an environment that is highly conducive to calm concentration.

A Regular Pattern

While it generally doesn't matter when or how long you work, it is important to establish a regular pattern of some kind. Not only does this contribute to the feeling of being a "real businessperson," but it helps in managing work flow and maintaining a desired income level. For example, I work from about 7 A.M. to about 3 P.M. each weekday, and somewhat less on weekends. That results in a 40- to 50-hour work week, and since most of my clients prefer to pay on an hourly basis, I can calculate my anticipated income accordingly. Another freelancer comments, "I have had to make a real effort to work semiregular hours so that I am not working 7 days and 65–70 hours a week. I'm more productive and much happier. I think I got carried away with the 'flexibility' of freelancing." (This is a common problem, even among experienced freelancers. Without "official" times for starting and stopping work, they tend to work all the time. Establishing a definite time period in which to work can help avoid this problem.)

On the other hand, it is not necessary to adhere rigidly to the chosen work schedule. After all, one of the advantages of freelancing is that freelancers are not locked into a 9-to-5 routine. When deadlines loom, I may extend my workday by an hour or two. On rainy mornings, I may get up a bit later. Every once in a while I may even take a day off! (More on this later.)

Breaking Up the Workday

In addition to achieving a balance between regularity and flexibility in work hours, it is important to divide the workday into segments in order to avoid the feeling of being chained to a desk. Instead of the coffee breaks and lunch hours of the office worker, freelancers use a wide variety of techniques to break up the day. Time set aside for meditation or prayer, or to listen to favorite radio or television programs, is often mentioned as an important part of a freelancer's day. One freelancer takes a midmorning shower; another reads a newspaper at lunchtime and cuts out the sensational headlines.

Taking a break now and then has a number of advantages. It clears the head and rests the eyes. It can relieve writer's block. It establishes a boundary between different projects if, like many freelancers, you work on more than one job at a time. And it provides an opportunity to take care of small chores and errands—sharpening pencils, returning phone calls, paying bills, watering plants, going to the post office or the library, and the like. (One freelancer remarks that when she's having a stressful day she finds it soothing to go down to the basement to do a load of laundry, which doesn't require that she prove her competence.) Some freelancers mention that they occasionally take naps—an idea that I'm finding increasingly attractive as the years go by.

It is worth noting that sitting in a chair all day, while it may seem relaxing, can actually cause fatigue and discomfort. To counteract these, get up from time to time just to walk around and stretch a bit. If you are under deadline and don't want to leave your desk, you can reduce discomfort by doing some simple "desk-er-cises"; these are described in Table 2. For the yoga-inclined, a shoulderstand for a minute or two (as long as you don't have high blood pressure) sends blood to the brain and can help when your mind freezes up.

The long and short of it is this: Successful freelancing requires a judicious balance between flexibility and self-discipline. As another ancient Greek philosopher put it, "Everything in moderation; nothing in excess." Too much flexibility leads to inefficiency and ultimately to insufficient income. Excessive self-discipline can make you feel like a robot—or worse,

Table 2

"Desk-er-cises"

Neck

With your hands behind your head, gently tilt your head down. Hold for 15 seconds while breathing and relaxing. Next, use your hands to gently pull your head down closer to your chest. Hold for 15 more seconds. Next, gently tip your head to the left and right.

Shoulders

Tilt your head to the left, keeping your shoulders down. Raise your shoulders to your ears while breathing in. Lower your shoulders while breathing out. Next, put your arms up. Keeping your arms bent, move them backward so that your shoulderblades move closer together.

Arms and Hands

Put your arms down at your sides and sit up straight. Stretch out your fingers. Hold for five seconds. Next, make a fist. Hold for five seconds and relax. Next, rest your right elbow on a table. Use your left hand to gently pull back the fingers on your right hand. Hold for five seconds. Repeat on the other side. Last, put your arms straight up in the air, stretching as far up as you can.

Legs and Feet

While seated, extend one leg straight out, off the floor. Flex your foot up and down, then rotate it at the ankle, making circles clockwise and counterclockwise. Repeat with the other leg.

a slave to work. And it is to avoid these feelings that we decide to freelance in the first place.

3
Maintaining Self-Discipline

Now to the nitty-gritty. As mentioned earlier, self-discipline (combined with flexibility) is at the core of successful freelancing. And the basic framework for self-discipline is created by a regular routine. Such a routine isn't established for you by the office environment. You need to create it yourself by developing a regular pattern for meals, errands, exercise, and the like.

To begin with, it's important to actually *start* your workday. If you work in-house, this happens automatically because
you have to get to work at a certain time. Sure, you may go get
a cup of coffee and chat with colleagues for a while, and perhaps read the paper at your desk, but if you don't eventually
get down to work someone's going to notice—most likely your
boss. So you have an incentive to start working. At home, no
one will notice if you laze around until noon and then do only
a couple of hours of work. But the results will show up in the
form of reduced income. Bearing that in mind, you need to
formally start your workday at a particular time or within a
specific range of times.

I find that starting the workday is relatively simple: I get
up, have breakfast, and go to my desk. This happens at 6:30 or
7 A.M., before the paper is delivered or anyone else in the house is
up. So there are no distractions and I can work intensively during the early morning hours—the time when I work best. Because I have to walk the dog after an hour or two, that forces me
to get dressed. Walking the dog provides a nice break, and I
come back refreshed and ready to continue working.

For me, the problems come later, when various distractions crop up and I get tired of working. For others, the reverse
pattern may hold. They feel comfortable with a workday that
starts in midmorning and extends through the afternoon. Still
others may not start working until midafternoon or evening.
The point is that they follow a regular, planned pattern.

Which brings us to the subject of procrastination.

Avoiding Procrastination

Many freelancers start their workday by—let's admit it—procrastinating: reading one or more newspapers, making phone
calls, writing letters, staring at the piles of papers on their
desks, having another cup of coffee, taking a walk (or walking
the dog). Procrastination can be the downfall of a freelancer.
It's so easy to say, "I'll start work as soon as I've done the cross-

word puzzle," or "I'd better go to the supermarket in the morning, before it gets crowded." Before you know it, it's lunchtime. Then a friend calls and you get to talking. Or you realize that you need to run out to the cleaners. The end result: fewer hours in which to work and earn income.

The best way to deal with a tendency to procrastinate is to make choices. Don't just drift through the day, idling over a cup of coffee, taking a shower, having another cup of coffee—and finally getting to work at noon (unless you're sure such a pattern works for you). You need to decide how much time can be devoted to such activities and plan them for specific times. You can put the crossword puzzle aside and do it during your lunch break; you can keep the TV turned off until the 6 o'clock news. The point is that these need to be *conscious* choices; otherwise your work time will evaporate. For example, one freelancer notes that she has managed to break the habit of waiting too long to start a project. Her solution: Break the project into smaller parts and set short, manageable deadlines for the small portions. Using this approach, she has even been able to complete a job ahead of schedule.

Some people may not be working under these constraints. If your spouse earns enough to support the entire household, and if you don't have to care for young children or pay college tuitions, freelancing may be more of an avocation than a business. But such cases are unusual in this era of dual-income households. And even if the profit motive is secondary, no client wants to hire someone who doesn't take the assignment seriously.

So how does the dedicated, hardworking freelancer begin the day's work? "The hardest part is getting started," says one. "I sort of sidle up on the work," says another. But there are many others who prepare for work by making lists, setting priorities, and organizing (or clearing) their desks and files. One freelancer starts the day by reading dictionaries, style manuals, newspapers, and reference books. Others begin by doing undemanding work such as recordkeeping. "To get in the mood," says one, "I fill out the Federal Express airbill and write out the invoice, with costs/hours to be filled in later. By the time these tasks have been accomplished, I've settled down and my mind has been geared toward work."

Mary Ratcliffe, an experienced freelance writer and desk-top designer, says that she can't start work until she is "show-ered, shampooed, and mascara'd. I don't know why, but the mascara makes a difference." She also has to move the cat. "My whole day, sometimes, is spent shifting a cat. While I'm work-ing at the computer station, a cat will settle beside me on the other desk, under the lamp, stretching out over the papers spread in piles by project."

At the other extreme is a freelancer who starts working before she is fully awake: "Just after I wake up, as I lie in bed floating between waking and sleeping, I write my leads [for news features]. Then I go to the computer, put the story into it, and edit it."

There is also something to be said for taking a few min-utes at the *end* of the day to write down priorities for the next day. That way you have a ready-made agenda when you come into the office the next morning.

Interruptions and Distractions

Closely related to avoiding procrastination is dealing with dis-tractions. I have become so addicted to solitaire that I'm con-sidering removing it from my computer. Other freelancers are addicted to the newspaper or television news, or are constantly interrupted by phone calls from friends and relatives. Still others find themselves checking their e-mail throughout the day. (E-mail, with its sporadic reward pattern, is like a slot machine for some.)

To reduce interruptions and promote concentration, freelancers often leave their answering machines on and screen incoming calls, or they turn off the ringer on the phone or simply don't answer it. Some tell nonbusiness callers that they're working and will call them back. (One remarks, "Now my friends don't dare call before 3:00 P.M.! I was forced to be stern.") They may also leave a message on the answering machine: "I can't talk to you now because I am deep in concentration. Leave a message and I'll call you later." One freelancer has an unlisted office phone number that she gives only to people who need to use it.

Some freelancers comment that it's important to close the office door—perhaps the shutters as well. One long-time freelancer sums up this approach succinctly: "No radio, TV, kids, pets, or chatterboxes in the immediate area." Other ways of promoting concentration—especially for writers—include pacing around the house or apartment and lying on the floor for a few minutes. (Writers often note that a sortie away from the desk can actually contribute to productivity and creativity.)

Freelancers with young children have a built-in source of interruptions. One freelancer with two young children describes several techniques that provide her with periods of time for uninterrupted work. She pays a babysitter to care for the children three mornings a week; at other times (provided that her husband is at home) she may close and lock her office door. In the evenings, after the children are in bed, she says, "I luxuriate in the quiet and get some of my best work done." When she's on a heavy deadline, she asks her husband, who also works at home, to take the children to his workshop—"i.e., get out of Mom's hair so she can make the 5 P.M. Fed Ex pickup."

It should be noted that some freelancers welcome interruptions because they add variety to their workday. As one says, "When friends call, usually I'm glad to hear from them and take a break." I'm in the latter category—I like to hear from friends or clients, and usually have no trouble resuming work after a phone conversation. However, you may find such interruptions unsettling. If so, just ask the caller if you can return the call at a specified later time. Most people won't mind.

About Habits, Especially Bad Ones

Freelancers—at least those who have been at it for some time—seem to be creatures of habit. Many say that they find departures from their daily routine somewhat disorienting and even stressful. Some say that they have tried to break a habit, such as procrastinating before starting work, but with little or no success. A typical comment: "Under press of deadline, I once forced myself to not start my day by reading one newspaper, and I opted to save even more time by not poring over another paper that I read at lunch. The result: Disastrous."

A few freelancers have managed to stop drinking coffee or smoking, but most attempts to break work-related habits are unsuccessful. One freelancer tried to stop eating cookies while writing, but failed; another once tried cleaning house in the morning but realized after three days that she wasn't getting any work done. One veteran freelancer says that she has tried to get up earlier and get dressed sooner, "but don't often succeed at either of these." Another notes that she tries to start working earlier by promising herself an afternoon treat such as a movie or swim. "Occasionally it works," she says, but "usually I keep at the computer until it's too late." Still another, a confirmed night owl, says that she can switch to daytime hours when she has company or is on vacation, but then immediately reverts to her nighttime freelancing. (She makes a point of noting that she can survive in the sun and has not yet turned into a vampire.)

Clearly, counterproductive habits, once acquired, are hard to change. One freelancer says that he's still trying to break the bad habit of accepting lower-paying work just in case higher-paying jobs don't come in (but they almost always do). Since such habits can have a significant effect on income over the long term, it is important to be aware of them and to avoid letting them become too deeply entrenched.

Taking Time Off

The typical freelancer works almost constantly as long as there's work to be done. Part of the reason is the pressure to meet deadlines, but much of it stems from just plain compulsiveness. Especially when one is paid by the hour, the urge to work as many hours as possible is strong. As one freelancer puts it, "I work Monday to Sunday from 9 to 9, with time off whenever I can grasp it. I'm trying to take more time off, but it's a constant struggle." Another freelancer notes that she works "as many hours as possible between 7:30 A.M. and midnight!"

While self-discipline is extremely important, it can become too much of a good thing. Freelancers who are chained to their desks for hour after hour, day after day, might just as well be punching a time clock and working on an assembly line. They are simply recreating the 9-to-5 workday. It's true that time is money, but it's also *your* time. There is a real danger of becoming dominated by the need to make money, with negative consequences in terms of health and happiness. Don't become a workaholic; know when to let go. Take an occasional day off, or even half a day. Since many freelancers work seven days a week and rarely take vacations, a day off has a greater impact than it ordinarily would. Note, too, that longer hours usually result in little additional work getting done. If you don't believe this, test it objectively. You'll find that the amount and quality of work done do not increase in proportion to the amount of time spent working.

I have had some difficulty giving myself the gift of time off, but an experience I had one beautiful fall day has convinced me of its value. Blue skies, glorious fall foliage—and I had piles of work on my desk. "It would be a crime to take time off from all this work," I said to my husband. But the lure of a hike in a nearby state park was too great, so I took the time off. It turned out to be the most spectacular hike we had ever taken, and I have rarely enjoyed myself more. I returned home saying, "It would have been a crime not to go hiking today."

Related to the issue of time off is the question of whether to work on weekends. Many people with long experience at a regular job have developed the habit of using weekends for shopping, family outings, home repairs, and the like. When they go freelance, they still tend to view Saturday and Sunday as different from other days. If the habit of working full time for five days and reserving the weekend for other pursuits is strongly entrenched, it may be difficult to change and perhaps not worthwhile (provided that enough income can be earned on weekdays). But there are some advantages to working on weekends. One, of course, is that more work can be done and, hence, more income earned. But an even greater advantage, in my opinion, is that working almost every day enables you to work fewer hours on any given day. This reduces fatigue and frees up some time on weekdays for other pursuits. For example, my husband and I try to go for a walk every afternoon. We both benefit from the exercise and fresh air, and we can still work a couple more hours in the late afternoon if we need to.

Another advantage of working on weekends is that days off can be taken in midweek, when most other people are at work. A few hours of a sunny Wednesday morning can be spent lying on an almost deserted beach, a far more pleasant experience than joining the throngs competing for beach space on weekends.

Separating Business and Personal Affairs

An important part of maintaining self-discipline is keeping your personal life out of the office. The separation doesn't have to be absolutely rigid, but there should be some degree of separation. Otherwise business and personal concerns will interfere with each other. If unpaid bills are clamoring for attention, you may find yourself interrupting your work to write checks. Bills and checkbooks should be stored in another place, to be dealt with at another time. The same is true for correspondence, phone calls to family and friends, and so on. While it may seem logical to keep all your papers and files in the same place, there is a danger in doing so. That is because the IRS does not allow a home office deduction unless the space is used *exclusively* for business purposes.

Along these lines, it's worthwhile to have a separate phone line for business calls, as well as a separate checking account for business income and expenses. More on this in Chapter 6.

Pacing Yourself

A final aspect of self-discipline is the ability to pace yourself. If you are faced with piles of work one week and none the next, you will be stressed out during the first week and bored during the second. It is much healthier and saner to have a relatively steady flow of work. This means setting a rough quota of work to be done each day.

Of course, workloads will vary according to the type of work being done as well as seasonal and other factors. Freelancers who complete large numbers of small projects in a short time operate differently than those who work on relatively large projects over long periods. I am in the latter category: Since my work involves developing college textbooks, my projects may last anywhere from a few months to two or more years. I try to have about six projects in progress at any given time and to devote an average of an hour a day to each of them. When I find myself approaching the end of a project, I start calling clients and asking for a new assignment. Usually I'm back up to full capacity within a few weeks.

People who write brief articles organize their work flow quite differently, but the basic principle is the same: Be aware of the patterns and cycles of your work and make an effort to achieve a relatively steady flow of projects. George Milite, who writes articles for newsletters and periodicals, has the formula:

> When I get a project, I immediately calculate how much time it should take me. I measure this against my other pressing deadlines, nonwork obligations, and my tendency to procrastinate.
>
> Next, I set goals. I tell myself I'll devote X hours per day to a project until it's done. If I don't stick to that, I make up the time the next day.
>
> If I'm working on two or three projects at once, I switch off after a couple of hours, unless I find myself on a

roll. This keeps me from getting bored, and it also keeps me from getting sloppy.

Because I like to procrastinate, I give myself artificial deadlines so that I build in a bit of a buffer. If I've been dawdling on a project and someone calls me with a lucrative and interesting job that's got to be in within a day or two, I can't in good conscience take that job.

It's important to know which of your clients view deadlines as sacrosanct, and which ones don't really care if something's a little late. That said, it's still good to stick to deadlines—both for the discipline and for the fact that you can't bill the client until the work is done.

In sum, while freelancing is a highly flexible lifestyle, it can't be carried on successfully without at least a modicum of self-discipline. The successful freelancer develops effective work routines and learns ways of avoiding procrastination, dealing with distractions, taking time off, and separating business and personal affairs.

4
Creating and Presenting an Image

ONE OF MY FORMER clients had a sign on her office wall that read, "Perception Is Reality." She referred to it often, and once, when I mentioned that I considered it a bit harsh, she said something along the lines of "Wake up and smell the coffee!" Indeed, when you think about it she was right. If a client perceives you as sloppy, disorganized, or unprofessional, that becomes the reality for the client. There isn't much you can do about it other than be sure from the very beginning to make the impression you want to make. That is, you need to devote some attention to creating and presenting an image.

Naturally, the image you want to create is that of a competent professional. This doesn't mean that you have to invest in the kinds of public relations campaigns mounted by large corporations. It just means that you need to think carefully about the image you want to present and take the necessary steps to create that image. Those steps include giving your business an appropriate name, having professional-looking letterhead and business cards printed, and putting time and thought into developing an effective résumé.

Naming Your Business

There are several reasons for giving your freelance business a name of its own. One is that a name creates an image of an established business providing specific types of services. Another is that a separate name for your business helps you keep the business's accounts and records separate from your personal affairs; this is especially useful at tax time. A business name enables you to obtain a second telephone line under that name, as well as a separate checking account. And it will help you feel more like a professional.

Some freelancers do business under their own names, and that is pretty much standard procedure in some fields, such as freelance copyediting. But using your own name as your business name has the disadvantage of not indicating the nature of the business. One way to deal with this is to combine your name with an indication of the nature of your business, as in "Tom Jones Editorial Services" or "Mary Smith Web Page Designs." But you may also want to consider an entirely different name, one that not only indicates the services you provide but also has some appeal in its own right, such as "The Write Stuff" or "Webs Unlimited." Such a name may help you catch the attention of potential clients.

If you choose to do business under a name other than your own and wish to open a bank account under the business name, you'll need to obtain a DBA. That's short for "doing business as," and it refers to a document that you obtain from the office of the county clerk, usually for a small fee. You show the certificate to the bank officer when you open your business checking account. (Note that checks made out to a business name like "Webs Unlimited" cannot be cashed without a DBA.)

To apply for a DBA, call the county clerk's office and ask for information on filing a business certificate in your county. You will probably have to obtain a business certificate form from a commercial stationery store. After filling out the form, you'll need to have it notarized before taking it to the county clerk's office, along with a certified check or money order for the filing fee.

Letterhead

Often the first thing a potential client knows about you is what your letterhead looks like. Since first impressions are crucial, it is important to have professional-looking letterhead. Your letterhead should present all the necessary information about how to contact you—name, address, phone and fax numbers, e-mail address—in a clean, uncluttered format. It should be visually appealing without being elaborate. Avoid fancy typefaces and colored paper, unless you're in a profession where these are the norm.

If you have some knowledge of type and design, you may be able to create your own letterhead on your computer. You can also have letterhead printed up at your local printing and copying establishment. They usually have sample books with a variety of typefaces and layouts to choose from. Or you can have your letterhead designed by a professional designer. This will cost something, but if a well-designed letterhead helps you impress clients and obtain more work, it will more than pay for itself.

Business Cards

Remember the line from *Amahl and the Night Visitors:* "I never travel without my box"? The equivalent line for the freelancer would be "I never travel without my business cards." I can't emphasize strongly enough how important it is to always carry business cards. You never know when an opportunity will arise to give your card to someone who may be able to hire you, recommend you to someone else, steer you to valuable information, or prove helpful in some other way.

Business cards don't have to be slick or fancy, but they should look professional. You can have them printed at your local copy center, which will be able to show you samples of different paper stocks and type styles. It's a good idea to look at some of your colleagues' and, if possible, competitors' cards to get an idea of the types of cards most often used in your field. If you are in a generally conservative field such as accounting, you may want to avoid a flashy-looking card. In a field like advertising copywriting, on the other hand, you may want something eye-catching that conveys an image of creativity as well as competence.

You can also make up your own cards using pre-scored sheets for laser printers. Just follow the instructions on the package. The result will be plain but serviceable.

Résumés, Flyers, Brochures

As a freelancer, you want to ensure that résumés, brochures, and any other promotional material you send out reflect what you do—that is, your services and skills. This means that your résumé will be a bit different from the traditional résumé that lists previous jobs in reverse chronological order. Its purpose is not to document past employment and qualifications but to advertise and market your services.

Although your résumé should include your work experience, it should emphasize your skills and capabilities. After all, clients are looking for someone who can perform a specific service. They aren't likely to be interested in your previous job titles. What they want to see is evidence that you are able to provide the needed service effectively. The best way to convince them is with a skills-based résumé, also called a functional résumé. Such a résumé presents your skills and capabilities in detail. Think of it as an advertising tool. If possible, include a list of current or recent clients and indicate some projects you have completed for them. You can also list occupational and educational credentials, but in a less prominent position. Participation in professional associations can be mentioned, but don't list personal information such as marital status, age, and hobbies and interests. (A sample skills-based résumé appears on page 38.[1])

Conventional wisdom has it that a résumé should not be more than a page long. This is not necessarily the case, however. Many successful freelancers have longer résumés. What's important is what's in the résumé, not how long it is. Don't include your college grade point average or details about jobs you held many years ago. But do include a list of recent clients or publications. And there's no reason to be limited to only one résumé. You can have several versions, each tailored to a specific type of client and emphasizing the relevant skills and experience.

As with letterhead and business cards, the appearance of your résumé can make a difference. Be sure to check grammar and spelling carefully and proofread, proofread, proofread! Your résumé should be attractive but not overly fancy, and printed on good-quality paper. Attach a business card to each résumé you send out; if the résumé itself is filed or discarded, the business card may be kept in another place, such as a Rolodex.[2] Again, you should follow up with a phone call after a few days. Even if no work is forthcoming right away, the

---

1. Detailed guidelines for creating a functional résumé are presented in Sheila Buff, *Résumés for Freelancers* (New York: Editorial Freelancers Association, 1996).

2. Blank Rolodex cards are available in sheets of eight for laser printers. You can print up a batch and clip them to résumés instead of business cards.

MARY RATCLIFFE • CORPORATE COMMUNICATIONS
304 West 75th Street • New York, NY 10023 • (212) 787-3974

SUMMARY

Versatile writer/editor/designer experienced in the creation and production of brochures, newsletters, product collaterals, news releases, sales promotion pieces, advertising copy, and more. Easy-to-read prose that demystifies industry-specific jargon and makes technical information accessible to lay readers is a specialty.

Graphic design aptitude and training enhance desktop publishing capability. Proficient in PC page layout, illustration, and word processing.

CLIENTS/
EMPLOYERS
(selected)

Takeda U.S.A., Inc./Takeda Chemical Industries, Ltd.
Japan's largest pharmaceutical manufacturer and subsidiary

Thoroughbred Retirement Foundation, Inc. (TRF)
Nonprofic humane organization

Macmillan Publishing Company
Collier Books

Koehler Iversen Inc.
Full service advertising/public relations agency

SIECUS (Sex Information & Education Council of the U.S.)
Nonprofit national information agency for health professionals

Lee Nordness Galleries, Inc.
Exhibition gallery; consultants to corporate collectors

Cinema Sound, Ltd.
Radio syndicator

Gale Research, Inc.
Publishers of business reference books

HIGHLIGHTS

- Desktop publishing design: writing, photography—TRF fundraising newsletter with circulation of 1,500 has raised as much as $16,000 with a single issue.
  Takeda USA company newsletter is distributed to subsidiaries worldwide.
  VitaminNews quarterly is distributed to food, pharmaceutical, and nutritional supplement industries.

- Product collaterals support $150 million in annual sales for Takeda USA. Artists' exhibition catalogs are preserved in Archives of American Art.

- Business-to-business ads have been ranked in top percentiles by independent recognition/recall studies; received award for "most noticed ad" from *Food Engineering,* a leading trade journal.

- News releases for clients are carried by trade and consumer press.

- Direct mail promotions resulted in SIECUS's first income-producing professional conferences and increased sales of their publications.

- Speeches for Takeda (Japan) management include chairman's address at international health symposium, Royal College of Physicians, London.

- Broadcast copy for INFO RADIO—condensations of consumer magazine articles (*Popular Photography, Stereo Review, Car and Driver, The Robb Report,* others)—was carried by over three hundred stations nationwide.

- Researched and wrote series of articles for *Encyclopedia of American Industries.*

PERSONAL

Member: Editorial Freelancers Association

client is more likely to remember you and may encourage you to call again in a month or two.

Sometimes a flyer or brochure is more effective than a résumé. It is more attractive, and you can include more information without overwhelming the reader. A brochure enables you to list recent projects and clients as well as your skills and services. You can also include testimonials by satisfied clients.

Brochure forms with interesting designs already printed on them are available from companies like Paper Direct. You can choose from a wide range of designs. For example, if you provide an international service, you might choose a brochure with a maplike border; if you provide services to book publishers, you might choose one with books lined up along the top and bottom.

Postcards and Newsletters

Some freelancers make regular mailings to existing and potential clients. This may take the form of a laser-printed postcard with news about what the freelancer has been doing and what new services are available. (A web site can be updated regularly also, but of course there's no guarantee that clients will look at it.) It could also take the form of a more elaborate newsletter, provided that there's enough news and other material to justify the greater expense. The lead article in the newsletter should be on a general topic of interest to clients; news about your own doings would go on the inside pages. Try to give clients something useful, such as "Ten Tips for Reducing Mailing Costs" or "How to Avoid Being Audited by the IRS." It's a good idea to write a personal note on each copy and hand address it, thereby indicating that you are a small business that gives its clients personal attention.

5
Organizing Yourself

THERE ARE THOSE WHO pride themselves on the disorder with which they surround themselves. Their desks are piled high with papers, mail (opened and unopened), bills, catalogs, notes to themselves, and the paraphernalia of their profession. Their answering machines and e-mail overflow with unanswered messages. They are constantly hunting through piles of stuff ("gnurr," my husband calls it) for that one item that has to be acted upon at once. Yet they claim that they know exactly where everything is and that they have no need to be better organized. "I don't worry about anything on my desk unless it jumps up and bites me," says a friend.

While some people revel in disorganization, others are overwhelmed by it. The sight of their overloaded desks fills them with dismay. They miss deadlines. Their bills are unpaid, their mail and messages unanswered. They are constantly saying things like "Someday I've got to get organized" as the piles on their desks grow ever higher. Procrastination sets in, and work doesn't get done.

If you sincerely believe that you can function effectively while surrounded by a disorganized jumble, that it doesn't impair the quality of your work or your ability to meet deadlines, all I can say is more power to you. You can skip this chapter. But frankly, I don't believe that there is any connection between disorganization and effectiveness. As any management text will tell you, effectiveness is closely related to efficiency. Efficient people get more work done faster, and this translates into more income, not to mention more free time. And efficiency and organization go hand in hand.

This is not about neatness. I'm not recommending obsesssive-compulsive or "control freak" behavior, although I will admit to being moderately compulsive myself. What I'm saying is that for a freelancer, a reasonable degree of organization is fundamental to good-quality, timely work on a variety of projects. And it is not a matter of having enough space. With a little effort one can create an organized work area even if space is limited. All it takes is some logical thinking.

If you are just starting out as a freelancer, it will be to your advantage to organize your work space before you begin your first project and to make an effort to develop habits that will make you more efficient. If you have already been freelancing for some time and feel a need to "get organized," some of the suggestions in this chapter may be helpful.

Ellen Marsh, a professional organizer, says that there are no problems, just decisions. If you are facing a large pile of "gnurr" and feel overwhelmed by it, begin by identifying the decisions that need to be made. Is there anything that could be thrown out? Do you really need to keep back issues of magazines and newspapers? Do you have a place to file the paperwork for completed projects? (If not, create one.) And so on. Soon the pile will be a lot smaller and you can concentrate on the more important decisions. (Some of Marsh's suggestions for organizing your work are listed in Table 3.)

Keep What You Need Within Reach

When advising clients on how to set up their offices, Marsh emphasizes the importance of having everything you need within arm's reach (everything essential, that is). This may be easier for a writer or desktop publisher than for a graphic designer or photo researcher, but the basic principle still holds. Time spent getting up and crossing the room to get a sheet of letterhead and an envelope is time spent away from productive work.

In setting up your workspace, anticipate the need to have all your essential tools and supplies handy. Most people can accomplish this by obtaining a fairly large desk with lots of drawers. Shelves immediately above or beside the desk are helpful, as are filing cabinets and rolling bins. A swivel chair helps provide access to nearby shelves and drawers.

To avoid crowding my work area with work that doesn't have to be done right away (in my case, textbook chapters that I'm not working on at the moment), I store materials in another room that doubles as a guest bedroom. If you don't have the luxury of "extra" space, noncurrent work can be stored on shelves in another part of your office or, in very cramped quarters, under your desk. The point is that just as it is inefficient to have to get up to fetch something, it is equally inefficient to take up valuable space with materials that aren't immediately needed.

If in Doubt, Throw It Out

We all save things—newspaper clippings, birthday cards, coupons, and other personal items as well as business documents

Table 3

Tips for Organizing Your Work

* Separate your workspace and materials from your personal space. Don't let them overlap. A separate room or a dedicated portion of a room is the best place to do your work. Allow space for your reference materials, files, supplies, and business-related accounts.

* Maintain a daily record of all business-related activities and expenditures. Indicate the amount of time spent on each assignment, including telephone, research, and travel time. Accurate records will document your charges and prove valuable at tax time.

* Set up a "tickler" file to remind you of assignment due dates and times for making research and information-gathering calls, follow-up calls, and cold calls to potential clients.

* Keep all loose materials in labeled files, boxes, envelopes, baskets, folders, racks, binders, or notebooks.

* Keep reference materials in a vertical position for ease of access and to increase the amount of horizontal work space available.

* Place within arm's reach whatever materials you need for each day's work, and work on only one project at a time.

* Clear your desktop at the end of the day. Facing a messy desk in the morning is guaranteed to diminish your enthusiasm and enterprise.

of all kinds. Some of these items will be useful—if not immediately, then sometime in the future. But we sometimes save things for no good reason, thinking that we should have them handy "just in case." These are the things that create desktop clutter.

Jann Jasper, a freelance writer who also trains people to gain control over their time and environment, has this advice for dealing with the paper glut:

> The first step is to go through everything on your desk. Throw out junk mail and any paper you don't need. Set aside reference papers—these shouldn't be on your desktop unless they are in use for a current project. Office supplies you don't often use belong in the supply closet.
>
> Now, all that's left on your desktop should be things pertaining to current freelance projects, urgent tasks, and pending matters. All these papers will go into your...working files.[1]

Jasper notes that it's necessary to be "brutally realistic" in deciding what to keep and what to throw out. "This may mean cancelling subscriptions for magazines we not longer read and throwing out announcements for poetry readings we don't really want to attend."[2] In making these decisions, ask yourself if you need each item *now;* if you could get it somewhere else (e.g., at the library or online); and if the world would really come to an end if you threw it away.

Working Files

One way of reducing desktop clutter is to set up a system of working files. I use a small frame for hanging folders (available at

---

1. Jann Jasper, "Conquering Desktop Clutter," *The Freelancer*, March–April 1996, p. 4.
2. Ibid.

office supply stores) and label a folder for each current project as well as the inevitable "Miscellaneous and Correspondence."[3] Anything that arrives on my desk—mail, faxes, phone messages, and so forth—is immediately put in the appropriate folder. Since I open each folder at least once a day (while working on that project), there is no chance that an important communication will be lost or ignored. This system has two important advantages: It reduces desktop clutter, and it reduces the feelings of pressure created by incoming mail and messages.[4]

The labels on your working files will depend on the nature of your work and other concerns. Possibilities might include "Phone," for calls that need to be made (but see the comments on working lists in the next section); "Reading," for newsletters and other items to be read when time permits; "Bills"; "Library," for things to be looked up at the library (but see the discussion of the Internet in the next chapter); "Photocopy," for things that need to be copied; and so on.[5] You get the picture.

It's important for working files to be readily accessible— either on your desk or in a nearby file drawer. If you can't reach them easily, you won't use them on a daily basis.

In considering what to do with each piece of paper, ask yourself what action is required. If the next action is to respond to a memo within the next couple of days, put it in the working file for that project. If the item contains supporting information that will come into play later in a project, put it with the other materials for that project, to be considered later.

Working files, of course, must be supplemented by long-term files. That's what filing cabinets are for. But they don't

---

3. There are other ways to handle working files. One is to use a literature organizer—a shelf divided into many horizontal sections. Another is to use wall-mounted plastic file baskets. Still another is an expanding portfolio with a pocket for each project.

4. More and more people are using computers for all this. Palm Pilot, for example, is a handy electronic organizer that has become very popular. If you receive lots of e-mail messages, you may also want to investigate e-mail filters and subdirectories.

5. Jasper, p. 5.

need to be nearby; they can be in another room, as long as they're accessible when needed. As with working files, it's important for long-term files to be organized in a logical fashion (alphabetically, chronologically, or whatever).

I keep an old office in-box near my desk and put to-be-filed items in it. When it's full, I take it to my filing cabinets and place the contents in the appropriate files. That way I don't have to make numerous trips between my desk and my long-term files.

Active Lists

Another trick I learned from Ellen Marsh is to keep a small notebook in which I maintain running lists. There are lists of the phone calls I need to make, the errands I need to run, and other things that need to get done. Each day I look at each list and decide which items need to be done that day and which ones can be left for another time. (You could call it "creative postponement.") The important thing is to keep the lists up to date and look at them each day.

The notebook can be used for other kinds of notes as well, and the inevitable small pieces of paper that tend to land on anyone's desk can be slipped into it and kept until needed.

You will probably want to supplement the book of lists with an ordinary appointment book or calendar. This can take any of a variety of forms, as long as there's enough space for all your entries. The appointment book can not only help you keep track of scheduled meetings, conference calls, trips, and so forth, but also serve as a backup to your working files. If you're afraid that "out of sight is out of mind," you can include reminders in your appointment book. (Calendar software is also handy. You can set reminders to appear on your screen when you start up the program.)

Along with my working lists and appointment book, I keep an index card listing my current projects. I check off each project each day after I've worked on it for the allotted amount of time. While this may seem unnecessary, it gives me an extra sense of security: I am sure that each project is proceeding on schedule. (If you've ever had that classic dream in which you forget to attend classes for one of the courses you registered for at the beginning of the semester, only to discover your error when it's time to take the exam, you'll understand why I do this!)

Organizing Your Time

Just as important as organizing your workspace is organizing your work time. (If you must procrastinate, limit this habit to non-income-producing activities like shopping.) The need for a (flexible) routine has been mentioned in earlier chapters and deserves further emphasis here. A routine gives you security: You know how much work you'll be able to get done in a day and can plan accordingly. The routine can be developed to match your personal habits. If you like to work straight through and reserve the late-afternoon hours for hobbies or other pursuits, this is fine as long as you can work effectively in the hours you have allotted to paid work. If you like the south-of-the-border habit of following a leisurely lunch with a pleasant siesta, by all means do so—but be sure that you are able to work effectively after rising from your snooze.

Organizing your time includes planning the time to be taken for meals, errands, and other breaks. Don't do these things haphazardly. If you don't keep track of the amount of time you're devoting to these pursuits, you may find that you're spending too much time away from your desk and not getting enough work done.

If you have young children, organizing time takes on added dimensions. Many freelancers try to work while their children are in the house, perhaps sleeping or playing in another room, only to find that the kids are constantly interrupting them and demanding attention. However convenient it might seem to be able to work at home when one's children are in their pre-school years, experience has shown that this is rarely a success.

In order to have several hours in which to work without inter-
ruption, the freelancer must make arrangements for the children to be somewhere else, or at least in someone else's care.
This problem can be approached in a variety of ways. If the
freelancer's spouse is available for child care a few hours a
day, costs can be kept down. Otherwise, a good nursery school
or nanny (or both)—or perhaps an exchange program with
other parents—may be necessary. Regardless of the specific
arrangements, the point is that serious freelancing requires
several hours a day of uninterrupted time, and this fact should
be recognized from the beginning.

One final note regarding organizing your time: Unless you
enjoy housework, a good housecleaning service is a worthwhile
investment. Just do the arithmetic. How much does the service
cost per hour? How much can you earn in an hour? Chances are,
the latter number is higher than the former, justifying the investment. Not to mention the fact that time spent working is
more satisfying than time spent mopping floors.

On the other hand, house cleaning is good exercise and
can serve as a way of preparing the mind for work. One
freelancer says that she usually tidies up her apartment for
half an hour or so before starting work in the morning. She
believes that cleaning up the physical environment helps
straighten out the mental clutter as well.

If you choose not to invest in a service but don't want to
spend a lot of time on house cleaning, you might want to look
at the chapter on "Sixty-Second Housecleaning" in *Working
From Home,* by Paul and Sarah Edwards. Not only does it
contain a number of useful tips,but it includes one of the most
liberating passages I've ever read:

> For some people "clean" means there isn't a lot
> of "stuff" around. For others, it means an ab-
> sence of dust or dirt. Take notice of what both-
> ers you and what makes you feel good. If it
> bothers you, you deserve to take care of it for
> your own benefit. So do it. If it doesn't bother

you—as long as it's not detracting in any way from
the success of your business—let it go and get on
with what does matter in your life.[6]

'Nuff said!

---

6. Paul and Sarah Edwards, *Working From Home: Everything You Need to Know About Living and Working Under the Same Roof,* 4th ed. (New York: Putnam, 1994), pp. 394–395. This comprehensive book contains useful information on a variety of topics of interest to freelancers. See the Appendix for further details.

6
Making Your
Work Easier

THERE ARE MANY WAYS of making your work easier; these include the various ways of getting comfortable described earlier as well as the organizational techniques described in the preceding chapter. But some of the most important involve equipment—specifically, answering machines, fax machines, computers, and copiers.

Although people who are setting up a home business often receive a lot of advice about the kind of computer they should buy, I believe that certain other pieces of equipment are just as important as computers, if not more so. Chief among these is the answering machine. An answering machine is essential if you want to make sure that you consider every single project that is offered to you. Clients often "call around," looking for the first available freelancer to whom to assign a job. If you aren't home, they'll move on to the next person on their list. But if you have an answering machine they may give you a chance to respond before they call the next person.

Most answering machines will allow you to call in from a remote location and listen to your messages. That way you can respond more quickly to a client who is offering a particularly attractive project.

It's a good idea to have two phone lines, one in your office for business calls and another in a different part of the house or apartment for personal calls. You may want a third line for a fax machine and modem (discussed later). For some freelancers, such as photographers or models, a beeper and cell phone are a must.

Freelancers disagree about the desirability of call waiting; some believe that it is helpful in that it allows clients to contact you even though you may be in the middle of another conversation; you can promise to call them back right away.[1] Others feel that call waiting is intrusive and may offend the person to whom you are speaking (presumably another client). I have never used the service, preferring to handle one call at a time. But these days the point may be moot, since many clients are using e-mail rather than phone calls to contact freelancers. (E-mail is covered later in the chapter.)

---

1. If you are speaking to a client and don't want to interrupt the call, you can ignore the call waiting signal. The other party doesn't hear it, so they don't know that another call has come in for you. But since you are aware of the other call, you can conclude the current call more quickly if you think the second call is business-related.

There are also voice mail services, comparable in cost to answering machines, that will pick up when your line is busy as well as when you don't answer.

Fax Machines

For many years I resisted purchasing a fax machine, feeling that it would cost money, take up space, and not be used much. I was finally convinced of its necessity, and I have never regretted the investment. In this day and age people expect speedy communication, and letters and memos are as likely to be faxed as they are to be sent the old-fashioned way. I still believe that a fax machine is essential,[2] but before buying one you should consider the possibility of investing in a computer that includes fax capability. (Note that computer faxes can send only material that is in the form of a computer file; documents not stored in the computer cannot be transmitted in this way.)

As the preceding comment indicates, the newest personal computers can perform many functions that were formerly carried out using other types of equipment, such as typewriters and fax machines. This being the case, it is worthwhile to give serious thought to investing in a computer if you have not already done so.

Computers and the Freelancer

Chances are that you already have a computer and know how to use it. If so, you can skip this section. However, some people are put off by the idea of using a computer when they're doing just fine with a typewriter or other tools of their trade. The mere mention of computers, with their high-tech aura and associated

---

2. A must for freelancers who receive a lot of work by fax and also need to travel is a fax machine that can save received faxes in memory. This allows you to download them into your computer while you are away.

jargon, may cause some freelancers to tune out. Experienced, hardworking freelancers may also feel miffed at the suggestion that they are behind the times, not with it, or just plain dumb if they don't run to the nearest computer store and shell out a couple of thousand dollars for fancy equipment whose utility is not immediately evident.

It doesn't have to be like that. With a little luck and some persistence, a freelancer can find information and advice that is not bogged down in technical jargon and clearly spells out the benefits of the computer as a tool. Neophytes should feel free to ask questions and not be snowed by the seemingly exhaustive knowledge of the experts. Even the experts were neophytes once.

Your Silent Business Partner. Freelancing is a business, and the desktop computer is a tool that can make many aspects of that business infinitely easier. The specific ways in which a freelancer uses a computer will depend on what kind of work that person does: A computer is invaluable to a writer, but not much use to a proofreader. But whether computer use is central to your work or not, you can think of the computer as a silent partner in your freelance business. Your computer can help you get work by producing high-quality letters, résumés, flyers, and promotional mailings. For example, with a computer you can tailor your résumé to the specific needs of each potential client. You can reuse whole blocks of text without retyping, adding only material that is relevant to the specific client. This enables you to send the same letter or résumé to several prospective clients, personalizing the information in each case. With a good printer, you can produce professional-looking written communications. The computer also allows you to keep copies of your correspondence in electronic form (which takes up very little space) instead of in file drawers full of folders.

Your computer can serve as your business partner in a number of other ways as well. With a computer you can keep a record of hours worked on a project, multiply the number by your hourly rate, and enter the figures on an invoice form, which you can print and submit to the client. The computer will also keep track of overdue payments and keep an accurate record of amounts received (which comes in handy when clients' 1099s arrive). And you can use your computer to keep track of your business expenses by category and even to compute your income taxes.

Pros and Cons. Most freelancers who use computers will tell you that the pros greatly outweigh the cons, but when you're just starting out it's a good idea to take a dispassionate look at the advantages and disadvantages of buying, installing, and learning to use a computer as part of a freelance business.

There are some disadvantages to computerizing, but for most people these are more than offset by the advantages. Among the most significant disadvantages are the costs: The purchase of a computer and associated software requires an investment that may run as high as $3000 (and even more for graphics-centered uses). It may be difficult to install the equipment, especially if there is no experienced person to help. Learning how to operate the machine and use the selected software may also be difficult without skilled, compassionate, hands-on instruction. Stories abound of people who have started using computers, spent several days writing a masterpiece, and then lost the whole thing by turning off the machine without saving the material. Another drawback, unique to freelancing, is that there is no in-house technical support to turn to when things go wrong.

Other factors also need to be considered. Computer equipment takes up space in the home office, which may already be overcrowded. And it should be admitted up front that not everything is speeded up by computers; examples include writing brief notes to oneself or others, filling out forms, and addressing envelopes. Many people find that they need to keep their typewriters handy for these tasks, thereby filling up even more of their scarce workspace. (But you can set up a printer to print envelopes and mailing labels, so there is no need to keep a typewriter around if this is the only reason for doing so.)

But consider the advantages. First, the costs of computer equipment and software used in a freelance business are fully deductible as a business expense. Second, as mentioned earlier, computerization vastly increases the efficiency of many functions, especially writing that has to be revised often. Computers provide improved recordkeeping capability and, often, increased freelance income. For specialized work in many fields, computerization is virtually a necessity. Indeed, for almost any "knowledge worker" today, the decision is not whether to buy a computer but what kind to buy—how powerful, how expensive, and so on—a decision that has to be made over and over again as equipment becomes obsolete.

Software

For the freelancer, the most important kinds of software are applications of various kinds: word processors, databases, spreadsheets, desktop publishing programs, integrated packages (which combine two or more types of applications), and a few other types, such as communications and graphics programs.

Usually a freelancer doesn't need a lot of software at first. You can start with a word-processing program and learn that before progressing to other functions. You can learn a program like WordPerfect on your own by using the tutorial included in the package, or you can get a friend to teach you the basics in about an hour and proceed from there.[3] Books and courses are also available. If you haven't tried it before, you'll soon find that it's a thrill to be able to write text, delete what you don't like, transpose phrases, correct errors, and so on with minimal effort.

Another type of software that can be a lifesaver for freelancers is the spreadsheet or accounting program. A spreadsheet allows

---

3. If you ask a friend or relative to teach you, be sure he or she is both willing and knowledgeable; otherwise the relationship may suffer. You will probably find that it's well worth the cost to take a one-day seminar or pay a pro for a few hours of instruction.

you to enter all your expenses in columns under the headings you will use on your tax forms—home office, supplies, postage, phone, books and publications, and so forth. At the end of the year it's a simple matter to add up the figures in each column (the program does it on command) and enter the numbers on the form. Income can be tracked in the same way and compared with the figures on your 1099s.

E-mail

Perhaps the most important function of a computer these days is to provide access to the Internet. Not only is a great deal of research being done on the World Wide Web, but a vast amount of business is being conducted by e-mail (electronic mail). In fact, e-mail is transforming the life of the freelancer. Many clients don't use the phone any more—phone (or voice mail) messages seem to be less effective than e-mail messages. Some people are much more comfortable with e-mail than with any other form of communication, and it is an efficient and convenient way to exchange information. Messages, memos, and even formal letters are transmitted by e-mail, and some clients and freelancers exchange computer files by this means instead of sending documents through the mail or by courier. Writers of short articles are especially likely to transmit computer files over the Internet. It's cheaper than faxes and faster than courier services.

Increasingly, also, research is being done on the World Wide Web rather than at the library. In fact, the web has been called the world's biggest library. Gaining access to the vast stores of information on the web can save you hours of time searching through library catalogs and making copies of material in reference books. (If you don't want to invest in a computer and modem, you can gain access to the web from a computer at your local public library—if you don't mind the inconvenience.)

The upshot of these trends is that it is becoming increasingly essential to have a computer with a modem, and to have

Table 4

Computer Terminology

audio—the capacity to output sound through speakers, record sound input from a microphone, and manipulate sound stored on a disk.

cache—a form of computer memory that can significantly speed up processing of some programs.

case—the unit in which the internal parts of the computer are contained.

CD-ROM drive—a device that enables the computer to access data stored on CDs (compact disk read-only memory).

diskette drive—a device that enables the computer to access data stored on magnetic diskettes.

graphics—any device or program that enables a computer to display or manipulate pictures.

access to a service such as America Online that provides e-mail and Internet access. In considering this investment, it is a good idea to check with current clients and determine their preferences. However, since most computers today come with modems already installed, there is no need to purchase and install a modem if you have recently bought a new computer. Just check the materials provided with the computer and follow the instructions.

Although specific guidelines on how to gather information about computers and decide on the right one for you are beyond the scope of this book, familiarity with some basic terminology may be helpful. Table 4 presents some of the most important computer-related terms, with brief definitions.

hard drive—a fast storage device mounted inside a computer.

keyboard—a device for inputting programs and data into the computer's memory.

memory—the computer's data storage facilities.

monitor—a device that displays images generated by the computer's video adapter.

modem—a device that enables the computer to send or receive electronic messages over telephone lines (the word is short for "modulator-demodulator").

mouse—a device that senses movements while being moved across a flat surface and conveys this information to the computer; also includes buttons for signaling the computer.

operating system—the program that runs all other programs on the computer.

processor—the computer's "brain."

Source: Gateway2000 Product Guide.

Courier Services

While fax and e-mail capabilities have cut into the amount of material that needs to be transported by nonelectronic means, there are still many times when you'll need an overnight courier or package service. The extent of this need will, of course, vary with the nature of your work. I have Fed Ex, Express Mail, or UPS at my doorstep almost every day, either delivering or picking up or both. For the most part, these services are very convenient and go to great lengths to keep their customers happy. It's a good idea to find out where their offices are, their hours of operation, and the costs of each. If you are going to be sending a lot of packages, it will probably be worthwhile to open an account with a service such as Fed Ex. This saves time and some money, and you won't have your credit card number traveling around the country on airbills.

There are many other ways of making your work easier, some of which are already familiar (e.g., copying machines[4]) and some of which haven't been invented yet. One thing to watch out for is the desire to buy new gadgets as soon as they hit the market, before you know for sure that they will be cost effective. When thinking about purchasing such devices, it's wise to keep in mind the classic admonition of Alexander Pope:

> Be not the first by whom the new are tried,
> Nor yet the last to lay the old aside.

---

4. Copying machines can be expensive and take up space, but if you live at some distance from a copy center, you may find a copier to be a worthwhile investment. If you're really cramped for space, you might consider a multipurpose machine: fax, copier, printer, and scanner all in one.

Occupational Hazards

FREELANCING IS A UNIQUE lifestyle as well as a special type of business, and both characteristics can give rise to a set of "occupational hazards"—or at least difficulties—that cut into the enjoyment that comes from being your own boss. For the most part, these are not major hazards—just bumps in the road that can be overcome with a little patience and creativity. But there is one significant occupational hazard that is faced by most freelancers, one that is inherent in the nature of the freelance lifestyle itself. It is the sense of isolation that comes from working alone most of the time. For people who really hate being alone, the freelance lifestyle can be very problematic. But for those who are flexible and adaptable, ways can be found to cope with isolation and even, at times, to benefit from it.

Other occupational hazards of freelancing are more directly related to the business side of things. They include the tendency to (usually unintentionally) provide free services to clients, the occasional situation in which a project isn't what the client said it would be, and the chronic problem of slow payment. But let's begin with the central difficulty: how to cope with isolation.

Coping with Isolation

One might imagine that a person who chooses to freelance is by definition a loner and must actually prefer to work alone. But this is not necessarily the case: Freelancing often involves a trade-off between autonomy (the desired state) and isolation (less desired, for most).

Isolation has two frequent side effects: loneliness and laziness. Loneliness because the company of other people is lacking and work proceeds in silence (except for the scratching of a pencil or the tapping of computer keys). Laziness because no one is cracking the whip or keeping track of the freelancer's productivity; there is no one to say that you can't spend the afternoon watching TV if you feel like it.

For some freelancers, loneliness is a constant problem and can sometimes produce depression. For others, it comes and goes or arises only under certain conditions, such as on gloomy days or when there isn't enough work. Laziness is not a major problem for most freelancers, but many admit to being easily distracted. (Ways of dealing with distractions are discussed in Chapter 3.)

When they feel lonely, freelancers respond in a variety of ways. They may sleep too much, spend a lot of time doing things other than work, or call people up. In fact, for many freelancers the telephone serves as a substitute for office chitchat. In addition, many keep the radio or TV on while working. They do not feel alone when they have a friendly voice nearby. One writer, who likes to have CNBC running in the background while he works, says that it makes his home office "seem not like a solitary prison cell or torture chamber but like a beehive of cheerful, important activity."[1] For him, the members of the CNBC staff are "virtual friends" who provide constant companionship.

For many freelancers, pets provide companionship and comfort. My dogs are always nearby, usually snoring but occasionally coming up to be petted or to remind me that they need to be walked. Other freelancers often mention their cats. Working with a cat purring in your lap can go a long way toward alleviating feelings of isolation or loneliness. Even birds and fish can have a soothing effect.

Some freelancers report occasional attacks of cabin fever, and they make a point of going out on a round of errands each day. It may be just to deposit a check or make a couple of photocopies, but it takes them out of the house and into contact with the rest of the world. This prevents the feeling of being a nonperson that can develop when one has been cut off from human contact for two or three days.

Besides dealing with loneliness and distractions in their day-to-day work life, freelancers must cope with the effects of social and professional isolation. In place of the social group of co-workers, freelancers may create a social life with a few close friends, become active in community affairs, or pursue a hobby with a group of fellow enthusiasts. Birdwatching and photography are great excuses to get away from your desk and out of the house. Clubs, committees, organizations, and other

---

1. David Owen, "Virtual Friends," *The Freelancer,* July–August 1996, p. 3.

groups enable you to get out of the house, meet people, and share interests. Lunches with friends, walks around the neighborhood, plays, concerts, and museums also provide needed stimulation. For professional companionship, associations like the Editorial Freelancers Association and Washington Independent Writers are invaluable. These offer human contact, validation, and the all-important networking that is central to any professional career, as well as helping freelancers keep up with developments in their field.

Another solution to the problem of isolation is to obtain a part-time job or to seek projects that involve regular meetings with the client or other participants. In addition, volunteering is a great way to deal with isolation. There is no shortage of groups looking for help, and in addition to providing balance in the freelancer's life, volunteer activity can be a way to enhance skills and meet potential business contacts.

Most freelancers agree that it is important to make a conscious effort to have some contact with other people each day. Many comment that it is essential not to let loneliness get out of hand: Before becoming overwhelmed by depression, call a friend and chat for a while. And don't forget e-mail. While exchanging electronic notes is not quite the same as meeting for lunch, it is human contact of a sort. (There is, however, the danger of spending too much time online, not only checking mail but also cruising interesting sites on the World Wide Web.)

Illness

Some freelancers feel that illness—especially something really uncomfortable like the flu—is a serious occupational hazard. When freelancers are sick, they face a hard choice: They can go on struggling to meet deadlines, or they can stop working and lose the income they might have earned for the hours or days when they don't work.

When deadlines are involved, there are several options. You could simply miss the deadline and explain that you were sick. (Don't feel guilty about this; bear in mind that it is a common practice among employees.) Or you could notify the client as soon as you are aware that you may have difficulty meeting a deadline, and get an extension. (It's a good idea to communicate regularly with clients anyway.) It's important to inform the client as early as possible when you know that a deadline is in jeopardy, and to be honest about it.

Many freelancers simply go on working when they're sick. One, who had hurt her back and couldn't get out of bed for two weeks, set up a system that enabled her to work in bed. She also noted that she works much harder after she has been sick—both to make up for lost time and as occupational therapy.

A surprising number of freelancers "don't get sick" or "don't get sick very often." For them, illness is not a significant occupational hazard. In fact, several factors operate to make freelancers less susceptible to illness: They have less exposure to the germs that thrive in offices and schools; they are subjected to fewer stresses such as office politics; and if they're feeling under the weather they can get some extra sleep and start working later in the day.

In this regard it's advantageous to have long-term assignments. Then it doesn't make much of a difference if you take a few days off. To cope with the problem of short-term deadlines, it's a good idea to build in some time to accommodate illness (and other unforeseen situations) when negotiating an agreement with a client.

One freelancer, who says that he simply works in bed when he's sick, notes that at such times he becomes more focused. Since he knows that he will not be able to do everything he normally does, especially the more creative tasks, he concentrates on a few specific tasks that he knows he can handle. He finds that he is far less subject to distraction under these conditions.

Being a freelancer tends to make one highly conscious of the possibility of losing income for unforeseen reasons, including illness. Some freelancers try to be alert to the approach of illness. When they feel a cold coming on, they take immediate measures to alleviate it. It can also be argued that it might be good for freelancers to be less worried about losing two or three days of income and to simply take time off when they feel as if they may be coming down with a cold or the flu. Taking the time to stay well will pay off in the long run.

Should freelancers figure on having a certain number of sick days and budget accordingly? I have a friend, a freelance editor, who records the days when he is sick so that he can factor this information into future contracts. This amounts to providing your own benefit plan. Another freelancer takes a somewhat different tack. He sets a specific income goal and works constantly to achieve it. If he stops working to recover from an illness, he compensates for the lost time by taking a shorter vacation.

Just as you're more likely to get the flu than to be disabled for a year, you are more likely to be disabled than to die at any given age. To protect against the consequences of long-term illness or disability, it is a good idea to invest in a disability insurance plan. These plans provide income protection in the event of serious illness. Of course, it goes without saying that health insurance, though expensive, is absolutely essential.[2] Just imagine what could happen without it.

Free Services

Another, often overlooked, occupational hazard is the tendency to provide free services to clients. Freelancers often provide current and potential clients with free advice, information, expertise, and effort. It's easy to provide free services of various kinds without intending to do so. Clients often call freelancers to ask for advice about how a difficult project could be handled. Or they may ask for time-and-cost estimates that

---

2. Often it is worthwhile to join a professional association in order to obtain the benefit of group health insurance.

may require several hours of work—and then give the job to someone else. Or they ask for the names of other freelancers in specialized fields. Or they take the freelancer out to lunch and pick his or her brain, assuming that the cost of a lunch is sufficient compensation. Or they keep the freelancer on the phone for hours talking about their problems.

In such situations the freelancer usually loses out. In one case a freelancer and a potential client met to discuss the client's needs. The client obtained valuable ideas and information from the freelancer, but when the freelancer submitted a bill for her time the client declined to pay, claiming that the discussion was just a friendly conversation. In another instance a potential client asked a freelancer to evaluate a manuscript and suggest ways to handle the project, a request that involved comparing several competing books as well as reading some chapters of the manuscript and reviewers' comments. This effort took most of a day and ended with the freelancer suggesting a specialist to take on the project; the client refused to pay for the evaluation.

It is, of course, legitimate to bill a client for time spent in these ways, as long as the client is informed in advance that a consulting fee will be charged. But how do you deal with a client, often a friend, whom you have known for a long time and to whom you give large amounts of advice, information, and assistance—not to mention time—without being offered a freelance assignment? Such services cannot be charged directly to a particular project, and in many instances the client would be offended at the suggestion that they be paid for at all.

One possible solution to this dilemma is to charge the client indirectly, by increasing the amount billed for a subsequent job. But this entails the risk of alienating the client as fees become higher while budgets remain unchanged. Should the freelancer simply accept the situation as a cost of doing business?

Some freelancers do just that—up to a point. They do not charge for the time they spend coming up with an estimate, considering it to be a normal business expense, but they will charge for a project evaluation. Or they arrange with the client to receive a consulting fee if the client later decides not to employ the freelancer. Or they take a gamble, hoping that a continuing helpful relationship with the client will eventually lead to a high-paying assignment.

There is always a risk of giving the client more than is asked for. "A common problem for me was a tendency to be too nice and want the client to be my friend," says Janet A. Smith, an expert in marketing communications. "I tended to give away the store. Don't ingratiate yourself. You're not indispensable." When asked what action to take if you're not being paid for what you do, Smith answered that there is always a danger of projects growing bigger than they were at the start because of numerous changes in scope. "The only way to protect yourself is to handle this up front by presenting contracts. If your client won't sign the papers, you can suggest they work with someone else."[3]

There is something to be said for the goodwill and credibility that accrue to a freelancer who is informative and cooperative and does not try to charge clients for every minute of time spent on the phone, in meetings, and so forth. The question is where to draw the line. It is important to be aware of how much time is being used in these ways and to make conscious decisions about how much time to give away and when the meter starts running.

However, there are some free services that are either taken for granted or so subtle that they are hardly noticed—yet they are time-consuming nonetheless. Editorial expertise is one area in which freelancers often provide free service without realizing it. Publishers are in the habit of assigning projects to freelancers without really knowing what needs to be done: copyediting, line editing, development, rewriting, or what have you. Often it's up to the freelancer to decide what is necessary and explain it to the in-house editor. Then the balancing act begins. The publisher has budgeted enough for a standard copyediting job—but the manuscript really needs a line edit. The freelancer knows how to per-

---

3. Quoted in Judy Sandford, "Keeping the Customer," *The Freelancer*, Spring 1994, p. 1.

form a quick line edit; the publisher will pay a little more, but not what the job is really worth. The compromise works to the disadvantage of the freelancer.

Training is another service that freelancers may provide at no charge without realizing it. Again using publishing as an example, younger in-house editors often lack knowledge about such matters as the difference between a preface and a foreword, and it falls to the more experienced freelancer to explain—on the freelancer's time.

Then there's the hassle factor. Consider this story. An in-house editor called a freelancer and asked her to evaluate a manuscript and determine how much editing it needed. The freelancer did a thorough analysis on the understanding that she would be paid for her time if she did not undertake the project. Then she was asked to edit a sample chapter (for an unspecified fee) and to provide an estimate for the whole book. She did so. Time passed; there was no word from the publisher. After three months the freelancer was asked to proceed with the job, but by then she had taken on other projects. In addition, it took several days for the publisher to get the entire manuscript together and deliver it to the right address. These snafus were followed by almost daily phone calls in which the requirements of the job were changed several times. Although the freelancer was paid for the job, the fee was not enough to compensate her for coping with these daily hassles and for shifting other projects around to accommodate the client.

Sample work is another dangerous area. It almost goes without saying that freelancers should never agree to do a sample without pay. Just as lawyers are not required to plead a free case and painters don't have to paint a free room or plumbers fix a faucet for nothing, freelancers shouldn't be expected to provide free samples of their work. Clients have the same recourse that we have when we're not satisfied with the service we get from a doctor or a car rental agency: Go elsewhere next time.

The attitude of some clients on these issues is an exploitive one: Freelancers need work, and the client will take advantage of that fact to obtain free services. If the freelancer were a physician, it would go without saying that the client pays for consultation time. But for many other types of freelancers the opposite seems to be the case: Consultation is assumed to be provided free of charge. As in most situations involving freelancer/client relationships, communication is crucial: To avoid being exploited, the freelancer must make clear from the very beginning that a consultation or evaluation fee will be charged for certain services.

Finally, it is worth noting that many of these situations are even more likely to occur when the freelancer works for an individual rather than for a company.[4] In such cases a letter of agreement is essential.

Slow Payment

Another occupational hazard for freelancers is slow payment. Since a freelancer's cash flow is likely to fluctuate even in the best of circumstances, clients who are slow to pay can really put a monkey wrench into things.

The amount of time it takes clients to pay will vary, depending on the size of the company, the efficiency of its accounting system, the amount of clout the freelancer has with his or her in-house contacts, and plain dumb luck. In publishing, for example, larger book publishers tend to pay more quickly than smaller ones, and magazine publishers and trade packagers are likely to be slow to pay.

Most freelancers believe that thirty days is a reasonable length of time to wait for payment, and that having to wait more than six weeks is unacceptable. The majority are paid between two and four weeks after submitting their invoices. The key variable seems to be the time it takes the client to put the freelancer's invoice "into the

---

4. Many freelancers comment that working directly for individuals can be disastrous. Such clients often do not pay well and lack a sense of professional boundaries. But as with most things in life, there are always exceptions.

system." One freelancer says that she often has to make several phone calls before she can get a particular client to take action on her invoices, and even then it can take several weeks for the check to come through. Another recommends that freelancers make a point of asking clients how long it will take to get paid. He refuses to work for clients who will not pay promptly.

I keep a record of the dates on which I have submitted invoices and check those dates from time to time. If I see that five or six weeks have gone by since I submitted a particular invoice, I call my in-house contact and ask him or her to check on it. Most of the time it's just a matter of slow processing. But sometimes an invoice gets "lost" (how or why is a mystery, but it happens), and either the client puts it through again or I have to submit a new invoice with the request that payment be made promptly.

When I refer to clients, I am speaking of companies, not individuals. Authors, for example, are notoriously slow to pay freelancers who work for them directly. In such situations it is advisable to have a letter of agreement stating amounts and dates of payment.

Another point that deserves mention is that many free-lancers value predictability as well as promptness. If a client pays slowly but regularly, the freelancer can expect payment by a certain date and plan accordingly. A regular cash flow can be a blessing for a freelancer, even if the flow is not as rapid as one might wish.

Maintaining Self-Confidence

Sometimes there will be lots of work, sometimes not. Sometimes the phone will be ringing off the hook and clients will be begging you to take on new projects. And then there are the slow times. When there's little to do and people aren't calling you up and making you feel needed, you may start to lose confidence in yourself, both as a professional and as someone who can earn enough to live on. This is a natural reaction, and I don't know any freelancer who hasn't experienced it at one time or another. Even more natural is the sense of shock and panic among first-time freelancers who have recently been fired or laid off.

All freelancers have occasional bouts of self-doubt and periods in which they worry about where the next job is coming from. These feelings cannot and should not be denied. What is important from a professional (not to mention financial) standpoint is to maintain the *appearance* of confidence and competence, no matter how you feel inside. For example, when calling clients, don't say "Could you give me a job?" Instead, say something like "I've been checking my calendar and I will be available for a project in a couple of weeks. Is there anything I can do for you?" or "I'm just wrapping up a project for X Client and will have a block of time free next month. Do you have an exciting project for me?"

It is very important to maintain a positive attitude with clients. Clients don't have the time or the inclination to deal with freelancers who strike them as inefficient or scatterbrained, nor are they interested in giving you a job because they feel sorry for you. Freelancers must always present the outward appearance of capability and confidence; if they do not, clients will assign projects to someone else. The old adage "perception is reality" is à propos here. Most of the time clients don't know you either as a person or as a professional, and it's up to you to convince them that you're the right person for the job.

Suppose that you've been maintaining a positive attitude and projecting an appearance of confidence for several weeks and there's still no work. Don't despair. Eventually you will hit the jackpot. Keep at it: Call every contact you can possibly think of and network constantly with friends and acquaintances in the same line of work. Persistence will pay off.

Experienced freelancers also note that it's important not to ask for low fees in order to get work. Underselling your services will not impress clients. And never sound tentative when you're looking for a higher rate (even if you're nervous inside). Simply *say* that you've recently raised your rate (e.g., from x to y dollars an hour). Unless the increase is astronomical, most clients will accept it without blinking.

Whatever happens, be philosophical about it. There may be some bumps along the way, but for the most part they can be overcome. It is always worthwhile to stop and remember why you started freelancing in the first place.

8
Health Matters

Unless you're a personal trainer or in some other relatively active line of work, freelancing is a sedentary activity. And like all sedentary work, it carries certain health risks as well as some benefits. The benefits of reduced stress and less exposure to some kinds of illness have been mentioned in earlier chapters. This chapter discusses some of the risks—but don't worry, these aren't serious risks; they're just health-related matters that should be kept in mind when considering freelancing. They're also important to people who have been freelancing for some time and haven't given much thought to the health-related aspects of their work. To give just one example, throughout my 30s and 40s I sat at my desk, writing, editing, and performing many other tasks related to textbook development, without realizing that I wasn't getting enough exercise. An occasional walk to the post office or hike in the mountains wasn't doing the job. Fortunately, I realized my error in time and joined a gym. The results were remarkable: My health and mental state improved dramatically, and I feel years younger.

Since exercise is the number one health issue related to sedentary work, we'll start with it. (After all, if you don't spend time maintaining your health, you'll have to spend time being sick.) Other health matters that are relevant to freelancing include posture, repetitive strain injury (RSI), vision, and believe it or not, food. (The refrigerator is always nearby!) These topics will also be covered in this chapter.

Exercise

Remember P.E.? Gym class? Calisthenics? By whatever name, I hated them and considered them a waste of time. Of course, like all schoolchildren, I had to engage in various kinds of exercise and sports, but by the time I reached adulthood I devoted much less time to physical activity. When the fitness craze came along, I thought it was some kind of yuppie fad, an excuse to wear spandex. How wrong I was! I—and millions of other Americans—now know that exercise is vital to a healthy lifestyle, and even more vital to freelancers who spend a lot of time at their desks.

The benefits of exercise have received widespread publicity in recent years and hardly need to be repeated here. Suffice it to say that exercise improves overall health and fitness and contributes to a positive psychological outlook. Especially relevant to the freelancer is the fact that it can also stimulate creativity. And it has great value as a change of pace from the routine of sedentary work.

The daily routines of experienced freelancers often include exercise, which may range from walking or running, working out, or swimming, to more esoteric activities such as snowshoeing, yoga, or Chinese gigong exercises (energetic postures to promote health and well-being). One freelancer with a dual career placed the following ad in *The Freelancer:*

> Ranya, aka EFA member Renée Fleysher, will be teaching a beginner belly dance class, which she recommends for editorial workers who spend all day sitting at their desks. All ages, sizes, and fitness levels are welcome. Improve posture and muscle tone, express yourself, feel great!

Of course, you don't need to do anything as esoteric as belly dancing to get into shape. Just join a gym. Most gyms provide a choice of activities, including aerobics classes, weight training, stretching and toning, and much more. If you can't afford a gym membership (though some are quite reasonably priced), you can still buy exercise videos for use at home, or lift weights (there are numerous books on the market that provide guidelines for working out at home). Regardless of where you exercise, keep in mind that it's important to pace yourself and to drink lots of water (not just while exercising, but throughout the day).

Exercise experts universally agree that simply walking— if you do enough of it—is all the exercise you really need. They recommend that you do a minimum of three walking sessions a week, each lasting at least 20 minutes (about the right amount of time for a break from freelance work; this is called killing two birds with one stone). They further suggest that each walking session consist of three parts: a warmup period, the walk itself, and a cooling down period. Basically, the warmup period

Table 5

Suggested Walking Program

Week	Warm Up	Walking Time	Cool Down	Total Time
1	5 min.	5 min.	5 min.	15 min.
2	5 min.	7 min.	5 min.	17 min.
3	5 min.	9 min.	5 min.	19 min.
4	5 min.	11 min.	5 min.	21 min.
5	5 min.	13 min.	5 min.	23 min.
6	5 min.	15 min.	5 min.	25 min.
7	5 min.	18 min.	5 min.	28 min.
8	5 min.	20 min.	5 min.	30 min.
9	5 min.	23 min.	5 min.	33 min.
10	5 min.	26 min.	5 min.	36 min.
11	5 min.	28 min.	5 min.	38 min.
12	5 min.	30 min.	5 min.	40 min.

Source: U.S. Department of Health and Human Services.

consists of walking slowly for a few minutes and then stretching for a few minutes. The walk itself must be brisk enough to deepen breathing and increase your heart and breathing rates. Cooling down means simply decreasing your rate of movement to a slow walk and continuing for about 5 minutes. Table 5 presents the suggested walking program developed by the U.S. Department of Health and Human Services, and Table 6 presents a "walking checklist" from the same source.

Table 6

Walking Checklist

1. Visit your doctor *before* starting any walking or other exercise program.

2. Choose a convenient time and place to walk.

3. Wear loose, comfortable clothing and proper shoes.

4. Avoid exercising outdoors during extremely hot or cold weather.

5. In summer, walk during the cooler hours of the day. In winter, walk during the warmer hours of the day.

6. Wait one to two hours after eating before walking. Wait twenty minutes after walking before eating.

7. Walk regularly: at least three times per week for twenty minutes.

8. Always warm up before walking.

9. Always cool down after walking.

10. Record your walking time and distance each day.

Source: U.S. Department of Health and Human Services.

Posture

Like phys ed or gym class, this is another topic that brings back childhood memories: "Sit up straight!" "Don't slouch!" Etc., etc. Well, once again they were right. Good posture is important to people in all lines of work, but it holds special significance for freelancers. People who sit at their desks for long stretches of time and do not pay attention to posture are at risk of developing

some rather nasty physical problems, some of which are mentioned later in the chapter. But let's be optimistic and assume
that you haven't developed any of those problems. You can avoid
a lot ofdiscomfort by taking some simple preventive measures.
The first of these is to invest in the right chair. Since you're
going to be sitting in it for several hours a day, it will be worth
the investment. (And of course it's tax deductible.)

How can something as prosaic as a chair be such a big deal?
Because while sitting may seem to be a relaxing activity, it actually requires effort—static muscular effort (in contrast to the dy-
namic muscular effort required for active exercise). Sitting involves
contracting muscle groups for long periods, which disrupts the
circulation of blood between the upper and lower body and causes
muscle fatigue. The strain created by static muscle effort may
result in pain in the back, neck, shoulder, or knee. Moreover, the
act of sitting places added pressure on the lower back, particularly when one is hunched forward.

To avoid these problems, you need to find, or invest in,
the proper chair. You need a chair that will enable you to
achieve proper sitting posture as you work. What is proper sitting posture? Here's what the experts say:

> Sit evenly on your bottom. Your knees should be
> slightly higher than the level of your hips. To
> achieve this, you may find it necessary to lower
> your chair or place a foot rest under your desk
> for your feet. If the back of the chair isn't curved
> inward to support your lower back, consider plac-
> ing a small pillow or rolled up towel at your
> lumbar curve. Keep your feet flat on the floor
> [or foot rest].[1]

---

1. Courtesy of USHealthcare. While we're on the subject, here's what they say
about proper standing posture:

> Imagine that a string is tied to the top of your head and is pulling you straight up.
> Tuck in your chin slightly. Pull in your abdomen, tilt your hips slightly forward,
> and tuck in your buttocks. If you must stand still for a long period of time, place
> your foot on a stool or phone book. This will reduce the stress on your lower back.

Of course, "the right chair" may be a matter of cash on hand. If you have $979, you could get what the Levenger catalog calls "the world's most comfortable task chair"—the Aeron Chair. The seat is made from the same mesh that Mercedes-Benz uses for its new car seats. The tilt mechanism allows the chair to pivot at your ankles, knees, and hips; the arms move up and down and rotate in and out—well, you get the idea. More likely, you'll be going to your local office furniture store to look for an affordable chair with good back support. When you do, take your time in making a selection. Don't be shy: Sit in all the chairs in the showroom if you need to, until you find one that feels good. Play with all the adjustments and make sure that you know how they operate *before* you buy the chair. And keep in mind the old adage that you get what you pay for. You may need to pay a little more than you had planned, but if the result is improved sitting posture (and prevention of back and neck problems), it will be more than worth the money.

RSI

Relatively unknown before the advent of computer keyboards, RSI (repetitive strain injury) has become endemic among people who use computers for a large portion of their work—which means just about everyone these days, whether freelance or not. RSI is insidious. It creeps up on you over a period of months or years, and once you have it there isn't much you can do about it. So if your work involves a lot of keyboarding, it's vital that you pay attention to the risk of RSI from the outset.

Deborah Quilter, an expert on RSI and co-author of *Repetitive Strain Injury: A Computer User's Guide* (see Appendix), points out that every person who works at a computer is subject to RSI. RSI is a cumulative condition caused by improper working conditions, and it has become so widespread that some experts refer to it as an epidemic.

RSI is defined as a "cumulative trauma disorder stemming from prolonged repetitive, forceful, or awkward hand

movements [resulting in] damage to the muscles, tendons, and
nerves of the neck, shoulder, forearm, and hand, which can cause
pain, weakness, numbness, or impairment of motor control."[2] The
impact of RSI thus goes beyond a few twinges and a little numbness. It can hamper your ability to earn a living and interfere
with your career. However, it comes on so slowly that most people
hardly notice the symptoms—which seem no different from all
the other minor aches and pains of ordinary life. So unless they
are warned in time, they may find themselves virtually crippled
before they realize what is happening to them.

Quilter notes that there is no quick fix for RSI; you can't
prevent or cure it by running out and buying an ergonomic
keyboard or by using a wrist pad or wearing wrist splints. Instead, she recommends a set of simple preventive measures,
which are listed in Table 7.

It's important to recognize that even two hours per day of
steady typing can cause RSI. The cause is not only the repetitive
motion itself but also habits such as sitting slouched back in your
chair and holding the keyboard in your lap—a posture that Quilter
says is "extremely dangerous for your wrists, your back, and your
neck."[3] Another really bad habit is trying to type while on the
phone, cradling the phone between your head and shoulder. But
there's more. Setting up a computer on a table that was designed
for a typewriter puts the keyboard and screen at the wrong level.
There's also what Quilter calls "human octopus syndrome," which
comes from working in a space where everything you need is
slightly out of reach. "People will be reaching all over and straining themselves in the process," she notes. [4]

RSI has a number of warning signs, including weakness in
the hands or forearms; fatigue or lack of endurance; tingling or
numbness; frequent, unusual clumsiness; stiffness in the hands or

---

2. Emil Pascarelli, M.D., and Deborah Quilter, *Repetitive Strain Injury: A Computer User's Guide* (New York: Wiley, 1994).

3. Quoted in George A. Milite, "When a Little Twinge Means Big Problems: Avoiding RSI," *The Freelancer*, January–February 1997, p. 1.

4. Ibid., p. 2.

Table 7

Ten Rules for Safe Computer Use

1. Maintain neutral wrist positioning.

2. *Never* rest your wrists while typing.

3. Use the whole arm to move the hand.

4. Keep fingers curved.

5. Use your strong fingers rather than your weak pinkies.

6. Use a light touch.

7. Work at a comfortable pace.

8. Take frequent breaks.

9. Keep your fingernails short.

10. Stretch frequently.

Source: *The Freelancer,* May–June 1996, p. 3.

---

difficulty doing simple tasks such as turning pages; tremors; and difficulty buttoning clothing or putting on jewelry.[5]

Other signs include difficulty carrying or holding things, wrist pain, and lack of control or coordination. Don't wait for these warnings to appear—by then it may be too late. Follow the suggestions in Table 7, and monitor yourself continually to make sure you are maintaining proper work habits. Not only will you avoid RSI, you will work more efficiently and comfortably.

There are some other devices and precautions that can help in avoiding RSI or allowing you to work more comfortably if

---

5. Ibid.

you have already developed symptoms. Some of these are a bit specialized and expensive, but they may be worth it in certain cases. Briefly, they are as follows:

- Use the Dvorak keyboard. It allows you to type faster than on the QWERTY keyboard and is less stressful on the hands.
- Use voice recognition software.
- Use the so-called "natural" keyboard.
- Use Pilot's "Dr. Grip" wide-barreled pen and pencil, which are specially designed for people who can't hold things tightly in their fingers.
- Get a keyboard tray that is fully adjusting.
- Put the mouse in your left hand.
- Use the telephone when possible (instead of typing a letter or memo).
- Learn to do more with the other hand, such as using the mouse and dialing the telephone.
- Type fewer words, make fewer edits. If you write more slowly, thinking carefully about what you want to write before doing the actual typing, you can avoid making unnecessary keystrokes. [6]

Vision

Like most freelancers, I depend on the use of my hands to do my work, so RSI is a real threat to my continued income-earning ability. But even more important is vision. To put it in the simplest terms, you need to see to work. So it's extremely important to avoid any problems of equipment or technique that could lead to impaired vision.

Of course, the first thing to do is to ensure that your workspace is lit properly. This means a high enough light level

---

6. These suggestions are provided by Robert Matson in "Writing Is a Contact Sport: Be Sure to Wear Your Helmet," *The Freelancer,* July–August 1997, pp. 1–3.

to enable you to work without straining or squinting. You can use either artificial or natural light (that is, daylight coming through a window), but I've been told that a combination of the two is best. Some offices try to achieve this by combining warm and cool tubes in fluorescent light fixtures.

If you do a lot of reading at your desk, a desk lamp is helpful. It may also help to use a slanting rack that holds your book or papers at an angle; several versions of such a device are available from companies like Levenger's.

And then there's our friend the computer. Most computer users will agree that if your work requires you to stare at a computer monitor for long periods you'll soon notice the difference between an average monitor and a high-quality one. I recently bought a new computer, and while doing so I took the opportunity to obtain a 17-inch high-resolution monitor. That cuts down considerably on the eyestrain that can develop after a long session at the computer. But remember, it's important to take frequent breaks if you use the computer a lot. If you can't spare the time to get up and do something else, look away from the screen frequently and focus on an object at least 20 feet away. (You can also do eye exercises: Move your eyes slowly in clockwise and counterclockwise circles, stretching at each number on your imaginary clock. This relieves tension in monitor-weary eyes.)

If you are concerned that cathode ray tubes emit harmful radiation, you can invest in one of the "micro-emission" or "TCO" monitors now on the market.

Watch That Neck!

While we're on the subject of monitors, it's worth noting that if your monitor is positioned incorrectly you can develop a stiff neck—or worse. Your computer screen should be at eye level so that you don't have to look up at it, and the keyboard needs to be low enough to allow you to relax your shoulders.

But freelancers can develop neck problems even if they don't use computers extensively. Like many people who haven't paid enough attention to posture over the years, I have arthritis in my neck. When my doctor informed me of the X-ray results, he noted that writers and editors are prone to this condition—degenerative cervical osteoarthritis, in formal terms—because of their tendency to slouch over a desk. So take heed! All those admonitions about posture that used to seem so boring were right on target. If you take good posture seriously, you can avoid some uncomfortable physical problems.

Another thing you can do to avoid neck problems (while taking one of those short breaks I keep mentioning) is a simple exercise. Tilt your head to the right and hold it there; then tilt it to the front and hold it, then to the left. Repeat the exercise several times.

If all else fails, I know of a wonderful heating pad specially designed for stiff necks. It's available from the Comfort Corner catalog, among other sources. You heat it up in the microwave for about a minute and then drape it around your neck. The pad is filled with "TheraBeads" that retain moist heat for 15 or 20 minutes. It's very soothing!

Food

Food a health hazard? You bet! Every time I've gone freelance after two or more years at an in-house job, I have slowly but inexorably gained weight. When you work at home the refrigerator is only a few steps away, and the urge to snack can be irresistible. (On the other hand, you are insulated from overstuffed deli sandwiches or burger-and-fries lunches.)

What often happens after you start freelancing is that you eat at numerous unplanned intervals. The result can be a change in diet toward more snacks and sweets and a slow, insidious gain in weight. You can put on one or two pounds a month without realizing it, until suddenly you wake up one morning and find that you're 15 pounds above your normal weight. If that's 10 percent or more of your total weight, you're medically classified as overweight. This can be harmful to your health.

There's also a tendency to grab meals on the run in order to put in more hours of work. This, too, can lead to imbalances in diet, since what is grabbed on the run is whatever happens to be available. As discussed in earlier chapters, it's important to actually take time for meals. At lunchtime, for example, take a half-hour to eat a healthful lunch. At the same time you can reward yourself for your morning of work by doing the crossword puzzle or something else that you like to do.

Another hazard is the ability to have an endless supply of food and drink at your desk. Many freelancers admit to consuming countless gallons of tea and coffee, not to mention cookies, crackers, and gum, while working. (It has been said that "an editor is merely a device to turn coffee into books.") One freelancer offers a solution: She keeps a glass of water in her office and tells herself it's a hot fudge sundae. This way, she says, she avoids eating constantly—especially when working on her specialty, cookbooks!

Naps

Recently there have been numerous articles in newspapers and magazines reporting on studies that indicate that large numbers of Americans, for whatever reason, don't get enough sleep. The researchers warn of negative consequences, such as (surprise!) lack of alertness on the job. Although they recognize that many employers may not be very receptive to the idea, they recommend naps. Yes, naps. Try it, you may like it.

Freelancers have more control over their time than people who work at "regular" jobs, so they can decide to get enough sleep at night by, say, going to bed at midnight and getting up at 8 A.M. (instead of at the crack of dawn to catch a commuter train). Or they can arrange their workday to include a half-hour nap in midafternoon. I find an occasional nap to be refreshing, but if you're the kind of person who tends to be groggy after napping, don't plan to do any creative work afterwards. Save your nap for late afternoon. Then you can wake up just in time for dinner and the evening news!

Avoiding Worry

FREELANCING IS WIDELY REGARDED as a rather risky way
to make a living. After all, you never know where your
next paycheck is coming from (or when). You can't be
confident that you will have work when your current projects
are finished, and when you do get work there may be too much
of it, causing you to work around the clock to meet deadlines.

If you're used to a steady workload and cash flow, freelancing can be a source of a lot of worries.

But this doesn't necessarily have to be the case. By keeping on your toes and applying certain basic techniques for managing your work, you can avoid worry and focus instead on getting the job done. This chapter covers several areas in which you can take positive actions that will help you avoid worrying about the less secure aspects of freelancing. Since a freelancer's well-being is intimately linked to relations with clients, we'll start with the client.

Client Relations

In freelancing, there is no guarantee that one project will lead to another. Your workload is entirely dependent on your clients' needs. If you get along well with your clients and satisfy their needs, you'll usually have a steady flow of work and, hence, fewer worries. There's a saying among freelancers: "You're only as good as your last project." This translates into a requirement that you must *always* do a good job on *every* project. It's hard enough to keep clients in today's climate of mergers, acquisitions, and downsizing. It's even harder if you miss deadlines or do unsatisfactory work.

Here are some basic tips for dealing with clients:

- Always keep the client's needs in mind.
- Plan carefully before you write, call, or meet with a new client.
- Send a thank-you note after an interview or to acknowledge a referral.
- At the beginning of each assignment, ask for a letter of agreement outlining the terms of the assignment—responsibilities, due dates, payments, etc.
- If you run into a problem, try to solve it yourself, but if that doesn't work, alert the client promptly.

- Remember: Clear, honest, timely communication is
  fundamental to good client relations.

In fact, the cardinal rule of client relations is similar to
the one about real estate, but instead of "location, location,
location," it's "communication, communication, communication."
This point is amply supported by the list of clients' pet peeves
about freelancers presented in Table 8. It's also expressed in
the following comments by one of my clients:

> Any time I spend explaining a job to a freelancer,
> especially if I have to labor over explaining ex-
> actly what I want—that's lost time for me. I'd say
> that a good skill for a freelancer is the ability to
> ask good questions. For example, what exactly is
> "urgent" (tomorrow, drop everything, or next
> week)? What is the preferred mode of communi-
> cation (fax, phone, e-mail)? And so on. These are
> the basic types of questions. Then the freelancer
> needs to find out as much as possible about the
> specifics of the job. Also, some freelancers put into
> their contracts what they are *not* going to be do-
> ing (e.g., writing marketing copy, telephoning
> reviewers). That's very smart.

Clients are looking for freelancers whom they can trust,
who are pleasant to work with, and whom they can depend on
to deliver the goods on time and at a high level of quality. If
you maintain these standards at all times, your freelance career will proceed much more smoothly.

Avoiding Money Worries

This heading might seem like an oxymoron, especially for
freelancers, whose income is by definition subject to fluctuations

Table 8

Frequently Cited Pet Peeves of Clients

Freelancers who go ahead and do a job without asking questions, especially questions about what exactly they are expected to do.*

Freelancers who don't keep in touch by calling or e-mailing to report on the progress of a project.

Freelancers who fail to inform the client when they are going to miss a deadline.

Freelancers who don't follow the client's guidelines for a project.

Freelancers who decline to provide samples or take tests to demonstrate their skill.

Freelancers who are so isolated that they spend too much time on the phone. Hungry for adult contact, they'll talk your ear off.

Freelancers who aren't realistic and flexible—who refuse to adjust their standards to meet the client's needs and fail to warn the client when it's necessary to cut corners on a job.

Freelancers who take a cavalier attitude toward schedules.

Freelancers who are given the name of a contact person but don't keep that person in the information loop.

Freelancers who repeatedly ask a question for which the answer is not yet available.

*This peeve has a flip side: freelancers who ask too many questions, who want to have their hand held instead of being goal oriented and displaying confidence.

and sudden shifts. But there are ways of arranging your business so as to be relatively free from financial worry. The first thing to do is decide how much you need to earn to live comfortably. Since much freelance work is paid by the hour, this calculation isn't very difficult. Find out what the usual rate is for the kind of work you do,[1] decide how many hours a week you are willing to work, and multiply these two numbers. Multiply the result by the number of weeks you expect to work (allowing for sick days, holidays, vacation, and other "down time"), and you'll have the amount you can earn in a year. If that amount meets your needs, the next step is to find enough work to meet the target. (This calculation is more difficult for work that is paid on a per-piece or per-project basis, but it can still be done.)[2]

Part of this process includes making sure that you're paid what you're worth. If a client is unwilling to pay that much, see if there might be a way to modify the project so that both you and the client are satisfied (example: produce a four-page newsletter instead of an eight-pager).

A trap to be avoided at all costs is to settle for a client that pays poorly because you don't have any other irons in the fire. Remember that poor payers are just as demanding as those who are willing to pay a decent amount. Hang in there and wait for a better opportunity to come along. Use the time to market yourself and your skills; make some calls, send out some résumés, do some networking. These efforts will pay off in both the short and the long run.[3]

It's important to be aware of what particular jobs are worth. This information can be obtained by networking with other freelancers in your field, as well as by simply asking clients

---

1. Every few years the Editorial Freelancers Association publishes a survey of rates paid to freelancers who do such work as writing, editing, indexing, proofreading, desktop publishing, advertising copy writing, and much more. This can be a valuable resource in determining how much you can earn for some kinds of "knowledge work."

2. See Laurie Lewis, *What to Charge* (Putnam Valley, NY: Aletheia Publications, 2000).

3. There is almost never any good reason to accept work that pays less than what you normally charge. For more about this, see Lewis, *What to Charge*.

how much they have budgeted for a project. Quoting too low a
fee makes you look inexperienced, so be sure that you know
what a given project is worth before committing yourself. It
also helps to have a contract or letter of agreement so that you
can anticipate specific payments at specific times.[4]

Managing Cash Flow

Cash flow obviously is central to the life of a freelancer. If it
fluctuates too wildly, you will experience periods of feast or
famine—literally. But if you are reasonably confident that there
is enough cash coming in so that you can live comfortably for
the next couple of months, you are well on your way toward
achieving worry-free freelancing. (Be very careful about using credit cards and other delayed-payment options. You can
overextend yourself before you know it.)

But how can you smooth out the variable cash flow that
is the inevitable consequence of not receiving a regular paycheck? Basically, by trying to approximate a regular paycheck in the form of project payments that arrive at more or
less regular intervals.

Many clients are willing to accept partial or periodic invoices, especially for large projects that are carried out over
long periods. I send out an invoice at the end of each month
for the work I have done on each of my textbook projects during the month. That way I have a pretty good idea of how
much cash I'll have on hand about a month later. Of course,
the interval between submission of the invoice and receipt of
the payment will vary, but over time you can figure out which
clients pay more quickly and which ones need more time, and
set up your agreements accordingly.

What happens at the end of a project? You replace it with
another one and start sending invoices after the first month.

---

4. Some of these ideas are described in Wendy J. Meyeroff, "Getting Paid What
You're Worth," *The Freelancer,* January–February 1996, pp. 6–7.

The trick is to replace projects in such a way that your work flow, as well as your cash flow, remains steady.

Managing Work Flow

Tips for managing work flow have been given in earlier chapters, but it's worth pointing out here that managing things so that you have a steady flow of work—not too much and not too little—is a major step toward worry-free freelancing. Admittedly, this can be hard to achieve. One freelancer notes that she is never satisfied with her workload. For example, one year she wanted to have a smaller workload during the holidays, but when the work actually started falling off, she began worrying that she might not have enough work in the future. In fact, this is a common problem among freelancers: Whenever their workload slacks off a little, they become a bit paranoid, fearing that it won't pick up again—this despite many years of cyclical work flows and familiarity with seasonal trends.

The solution to this problem hinges on self-confidence. You need to remind yourself that there will always be fluctuations in the flow of work—that any decline is temporary and sooner or later will be followed by an upswing. Under such circumstances it helps to talk to a colleague in the same profession; your shared experiences will help build confidence on both sides.

The other side of the coin is an overflow of work, which can occur for a variety of reasons. Sometimes several clients offer a freelancer attractive projects within a short span of time, and the freelancer can't bear to turn any of them down. Or various other participants in a project work more slowly than expected, so the freelancer ends up with his or her portion of the work at a later date than expected—and at a time when several other projects much be done as well. Whatever the reason, the "feast" part of "feast or famine" needs to be addressed as carefully as the "famine" part.

Some freelancers who are experiencing a work glut simply put in more hours or cut down on their social and recreational life. Others subcontract; that is, they hire another freelancer to do all or part of a job that they can't handle because of their heavy workload. Subcontracting can be an effective tool if you know and trust the person to whom you are assigning the job. However, it carries significant risks. One risk is that the client will discover that someone else did the work for which you were hired. To some clients, this doesn't matter; to others, it matters a great deal. They may have hired you because of your unique expertise and experience in a particular type of work, and may feel shortchanged if they find that the work was actually done by someone else.

Another risk is that the person to whom you subcontract the project will not do as good a job as you expected, and you'll have to fix whatever is wrong. This can take a lot of time, thereby defeating the purpose of subcontracting. Or, for whatever reason, the subcontractor may fail to finish the job on time—or at all—placing you in a difficult position with your client. In any case, you'll have to spend time checking the subcontractor's work— time that you probably can't spare from your own schedule.

Elsa Peterson, a photo and permissions researcher, has subcontracted work for many years but now tries to avoid it because subcontractors have often let her down. She suggests that if you are considering subcontracting you should pay attention to the following issues:

- Legal issues—make sure the subcontractor understands the assignment, and have a written contract that your lawyer has reviewed.
- Space—will the subcontractor spend much time on your premises? How will that affect your ability to be productive and comfortable?
- Insurance—homeowners' policies often exclude people who are on your premises for business purposes.

Of course, you have to pay people to whom you subcontract work, and this can pose some thorny problems. You want to pay them less than the client will pay you, but at the same time you don't want to exploit them any more than you would want to be exploited if the situation were reversed. This means that the difference between what you pay the subcontractor and what the client pays you is unlikely to be very substantial. When you consider the amount of time you have to invest in the arrangement, it may not be worth the effort.

Marketing Your Services

Of course, the ideal situation is a steady series of interesting jobs that keeps work on your desk and money in your bank account. One way of accomplishing this is to be constantly aware of the need to market your services. The ins and outs of marketing are covered in greater depth in other books (see Appendix). But because marketing your services is such an important aspect of managing work flow, a few comments are worthwhile here.

There are many ways of finding work. Most freelancers depend on word-of-mouth contacts and referrals, but these should be supplemented by planned marketing: placing ads, writing letters, and making calls. It is also important to build a client list. This can be accomplished by calling anyone you know who might provide a lead, including friends, business colleagues and subordinates, former employees, former school-mates, people you know in professional associations, and so forth. Company names and addresses can also be found in materials available at the library, including directories, trade journals, and other books and periodicals. And don't forget the phone book!

If you computerize your list of actual and potential clients, you can generate not only a phone list but also letters, reports, and invoices. (See the section on "Computers and the Freelancer" in Chapter 6.) Be sure to update your client list from time to time.

If you are planning to make calls,[5] wait until you are in the mood to deal with the outside world. Sometimes it helps to set a specific time for making calls and to dress in a business-like manner before calling clients. It also helps to make some notes beforehand so that you will be as clear as possible in explaining what you can offer to the client and what you expect in return. (It's OK to practice out loud!)

When you do get a chance to talk to a potential client, don't let your excitement run away with you. Sure, you've been looking for work for weeks and the refrigerator is empty except for half a carton of Chinese takeout, but the client doesn't need to know these things. Focus on the client's needs, your qualifications, similar jobs you've done in the past, deadlines, and related matters. Don't talk about your children, your pets, your health, or other personal topics. And even if clients say that they don't need your services, don't take that as final. Try them again in a few weeks. Persistence will pay off in the long run.

Visiting a client's office in person can be helpful, especially if you are just beginning to work for that client or have not seen him or her for a long time. This "face time" puts you closer to the top of the heap in the client's mind when it's time to assign a new project. Some consultants make a point of spending time in person with each client every few months.

It is also useful to be on the alert for jobs that might come from unexpected quarters. Occasionally freelancers' avocations come in handy in marketing their services. A freelancer with a passion for Hollywood films has been able to obtain work in that subject area; another, who specializes in Italian literature from the Renaissance period (including discovering and translating it), has become an author and formed a small press. A specialist in taxonomy once got a job advising the publisher of a major dictionary on taxonomic issues. A freelancer who is

---

5. Many clients prefer to be contacted by mail rather than by phone. This allows them to respond at their convenience. It is acceptable to follow up a letter with a phone call a couple of weeks later.

interested in building and construction has been able to find work with how-to publishers, while one with a specialty in Medieval and Renaissance literature edits texts and journals in that field. A writer with an interest in dancing in Washington has self-published a book on the subject; another, whose interest is in the eastern end of Long Island, does some work for a local paper. A performance artist has written two plays that were published in textbooks; a skier has written numerous articles for *Skiing* Magazine and is sometimes paid to ski in beautiful locales and write about the experience.

Continuous Prospecting

It should be clear by now that the best way to avoid worry as a freelancer is to continually market your services. If you wait until you're out of work before looking for new projects, a corresponding gap will show up in your cash flow a month or two later. That's why it's a good idea to engage in continuous prospecting.

One writer on the subject offers four practical points that should be kept in mind:

- Never forget you work to make money.
- You offer services and expertise people want; you are not selling something.
- If you don't get the assignment, don't take it personally. "No" simply means: Not this time. Try again.
- Hundreds of clients are looking for the services you offer. The literal definition of prospecting is to explore. Find them.[6]

Experienced freelancers use a variety of techniques and resources to market their services. As mentioned in Chapter 4,

---

6. Hovey Brock, "Prospecting: Key to Survival," *The Freelancer,* January–February 1994, p. 2.

many choose a name for their business that reflects what they do. They hire a competent designer to create brochures and other promotional materials, which are mailed out on a regular basis. They also allocate specific blocks of time to these activities—such as one morning per week. They follow up their mailings with phone calls to clients, just to touch base and remind them that they are available.

Advertising can be helpful in attracting new clients, but its effectiveness varies from one type of work to another. Ask freelancers working in the same field whether they advertise and, if so, whether they believe their ads have brought in new clients and projects.

If you have an account with an Internet provider, consider setting up a web site devoted to your business. Web page designers are widely available these days. Be sure to describe what you do, your services, and the various skills you offer. A web site may be a good place to provide samples of your work, such as selections from articles or a portfolio of photos.

Other possible sources of prospective clients include industry-specific trade association membership directories, trade association journals, membership in a trade association, referrals by current clients, former employers and colleagues, industry directories, trade shows or industrial conferences, and college alumni associations. (Make sure you're listed in relevant directories, such as *Literary Market Place,* so that you're easy to find.) Even family members and friends may be able to give you the names of people to contact, so make sure they are aware of the kind of work you can do.

There are many books on the market that describe the prospecting and self-marketing process in more detail. The point here is simply that you need to allocate sufficient time for this task and to be aware of the need to contact clients repeatedly in order to maintain a steady flow of work. Marketing should be done all the time, not just during slow periods.

In freelancing as in many other pursuits, finding jobs and clients often boils down to whom you know. Most freelancers can tell you about jobs that they found as a result of networking.

It is important to keep in contact not only with people who do similar work but with anyone who might know someone who needs the kind of work you do. You should talk to such people whenever possible, because you never know who is going to be your next connection. And remember to thank anyone who has recommended you for a job.

Next to networking, persistence is the most important factor in getting new business. Even if the person you are contacting doesn't have any work for you right now, he or she may be able to use your services at a later date or may refer you to someone else. This doesn't mean making a pest of yourself, just following up periodically with a note or a phone call. It will pay off in the long run—and possibly in the short run as well.

Some Minor Money Matters

Now that you have your work flow under control, you should be able to avoid major fluctuations in income. To smooth things out still more, however, there are some simple techniques that you can use—depending, as always, on the nature of your work.

Rather than submitting an invoice when you complete each project, try to arrange to submit monthly invoices if you're working on a long-term project. This works best for projects for which you charge an hourly rate; you simply submit a bill indicating the total number of hours worked and the amount due. If the job is being done under a flat-fee contract, try to include in the contract a provision for periodic invoicing—for example, every three months. That way you can gauge in advance the amount of income you'll be receiving in the next month or quarter and plan accordingly.

When charging an hourly rate, it's important to bill for *all* your time—not just the time you spend directly working on the project but also the time you spend in meetings, traveling to and from the client's office, talking with the client on the phone, writing memos, going to the copy center, and so on. It's easy to forget that you're working at these times, but experienced freelancers make a point of keeping detailed records of these activities. If the client questions these charges, point out that time spent on traveling, photocopying, and the like is time that cannot be devoted to other assignments.

Another area in which alertness and planning are helpful is in dealing with the IRS. Independent contractors don't have the luxury of automatic withholding; they must pay quarterly estimated taxes. Worksheets and forms for this purpose are readily available (you can get them by fax or off the Internet). Of course, if you haven't been freelancing very long it's going to be difficult to estimate your annual earnings. Try to come up with a ballpark figure to start with. In subsequent years, estimate your taxes as more or less the same as what you paid the previous year, and pay one-quarter of the amount every three months, using the handy vouchers supplied by the IRS.

I must admit that I took a rather cavalier attitude toward this process for many years. I wanted my income to earn interest (that is, if it wasn't being spent on necessities), and I didn't want to hand it over to the IRS early in the tax year. So I estimated low for the early quarters and paid the outstanding amount on April 15. The IRS doesn't look kindly on such behavior, however; it requires that quarterly payments total either 90 percent of the eventual tax or an amount equivalent to the tax paid for the previous year. After paying some stiff penalties, I cleaned up my act.

Most freelancers use the services of an accountant not only to prepare their tax returns but also to figure out their estimated taxes and determine their deductions. It pays to consult an expert. You'd be surprised at how much you can deduct as expenses (as much as 50 percent of your business income, according to some sources). All business expenses, including the cost of maintaining a home office, are deductible. (To take the home office deduction, set aside space to be used only for your business, even if it's just part of a room, and deduct a percentage of your rent and utilities.) If you are a member of a professional association focusing on your line of work, it can probably provide you with information about the types of costs and fees that you can deduct.

Be sure to keep a record of every expenditure; it will be worth it at tax time. The IRS does not expect most filers to keep receipts for items under $75, but you need to be able to document everything. The best way to do this, I think, is to maintain a simple spreadsheet like the one offered by Microsoft Works.

If you have an individual retirement account or a Keogh plan, you can use this to juggle your taxable income. You can deposit up to 15 percent of your earnings in such an account, and the money won't be taxed until you take it out after retiring (or any time after age 59½). The amount that you deposit comes off the top of your reported income, and your income tax is reduced accordingly. So if you anticipate a high total income even after deductions, put more money in the retirement account. Again, find a good accountant or tax consultant to help you get your ducks in a row. It will definitely pay off.

10
Taking the Plunge

THE THIRD (and, I now believe, last) time I went freelance, a friend said to me, "Freelancing—that takes courage!" I was astonished. I had never thought of myself as particularly courageous. (Foolhardy perhaps, but not courageous.) But to those who are used to the security of a full-time job working for a stable employer—if there is such a thing anymore—it may seem courageous (or foolhardy) to take the plunge into freelancing. It is, after all, a major change in lifestyle.

For me, going freelance again wasn't so difficult. I knew what I needed to do and set out to do it. However, someone who goes freelance for the first time may feel as if he or she is sailing into uncharted waters, with all the hazards that entails. But even people who have never freelanced before can set up a freelance business with a minimum of stress and strain by doing some careful information-gathering and planning. Most important, though, as emphasized in Chapter 1, is a clear-headed self-evaluation. If you want to freelance and believe in yourself and your abilities, the rest will take care of itself.

Although many people seem to just "fall into" freelancing as a result of other changes in their lives, it is better to start a freelance career intentionally and with carefully thought out plans. A key point here is that you should not go freelance on a whim or because you hate your job—much as you may want to. Like many other workers, you may be dissatisfied with your job, feel underpaid and overworked, resent having been passed over for promotion, and so forth. If you are frustrated on the job, you may fantasize about freelancing, but before you get carried away by the fantasy, be sure to stop for a reality check. It's also important to be realistic about what kind of work you may be doing at first. As a booklet published by Washington Independent Writers points out,

> If you stay in business awhile, you may get to the point where you're writing what you want. But in the meantime, there are bills to pay. Today you might be proofing *The Journal of Earthworm Science.* Tomorrow, you may be grinding out the annual report for the noodle packaging industry. And if you don't approach freelancing with a careful plan and strategy,

---

1. Carol Dana, "The Big Step," in Luree Miller, ed., *Going Freelance* (Washington, DC: Washington Independent Writers, 1992), p. 3.

Table 9

Decision-Making Checklist

- Explore your motives for leaving your current job.
- Decide what kind of freelance business you want to establish.
- Investigate your potential client base.
- Assess your financial resources and find an alternative source of income if necessary.
- Join a professional association.
- Begin contacting potential clients.
- Set up your home office and buy needed equipment.
- If you can, take some time off before starting your first freelance job.

---

you may well get bored—or go broke—before you've experienced its rewards.[1]

This chapter presents a few tips for easing the transition into freelancing. Some of the decisions required are listed in Table 9.

First, Decompress

If you've been working at a "regular" job (or series of jobs) for many years, going freelance offers you not only the chance to be your own boss but also an opportunity to take an open-ended vacation. You are in control of the amount of time you take off from work; you don't have to go back to the office after two or three weeks. Like a diver coming up from the ocean floor, you can decompress from the pressures of office life and begin your freelance career relaxed and refreshed.

A friend describes how, after her job evaporated as a result of a corporate takeover, she took a month to recuperate, regroup, and simply enjoy life. "I played," she says. "I slept in. I went to museums. I called up friends and had lunch or dinner with them. I went to the opera. I didn't worry about work at all!"

Of course, whether you take a few days to unwind or a few months to travel around the world before starting your first freelance project will depend on how much you have saved over the years (or, in this day and age, how much you receive in severance pay). You also have to bear in mind that you will not have a steady income flow in your first few months as a freelancer. You need to have saved enough money so that you can live without depending on freelance income. The rule of thumb used to be that one should have enough savings to be able to live for three months without additional income. I personally think that's not enough. I would recommend having enough put by to live on for at least four, and preferably six, months. By then you should have a reasonable flow of income and some idea of how much work is going to come your way.

Alternative Income Sources

If you haven't been able to save enough to live on for a few months, there are other ways to ensure adequate income during the startup period. One possibility is to work part-time for your current employer or find a part-time job somewhere else, something that is steady but leaves you enough time to do the planning and self-marketing you'll need to do to get started as a freelancer. Finding such a job may be difficult, though, unless you have specific skills and—especially—good contacts. I know a freelance photo researcher who works part-time in a bookstore, and a freelance copy editor who works part-time editing journal articles for a professional association. They work one or two days a week (so they are still classified as independent contractors by the IRS), earning enough so that their fluctuating freelance income does not create undue hardship.

Another source of income for a new freelancer is an employed spouse. This may seem self-evident, but it's important to bear in mind that if the household has been operating on two incomes for a considerable length of time, suddenly depending on one partner's income while the other partner establishes a freelance business could cause difficulties. Clearly, if you plan to live on a spouse's income during the startup period, you will need to make sure that the spouse approves of the plan. This is not the place for marriage counseling, but the potential for stress and strain should be obvious. On the other hand, I have found this to be an ideal way to slide into freelancing with a minimum of worry—and with plenty of incentive to find clients and projects fast in order to ease the pressure as soon as possible. A supportive partner also provides some of the psychological support you need while making the transition to freelancing.

Setting Goals

Once you have made the decision to freelance, and before you do anything else, you'll need to set goals. This doesn't have to be an elaborate process;[2] you just need to stop and think for a while before plunging in. First, decide what kind of freelancing you want to do. This isn't as straightforward as you might think Naturally, you'll want to do the kind of work for which you are best suited, whether it's a continuation of your present career or related work that uses similar skills. But this may also be a good time to switch to another line of work, something you've always wanted to do but didn't have the time or skills to

---

2. Some people find it helpful to actually write out a business plan, describing the business, setting goals, identifying the market for the business, and stating projected costs and income objectives. Personally, I don't think this is necessary, but you may find it to be a useful exercise.

do successfully. Such a move would require more effort—for example, switching from computer programming to photography might entail taking some courses and investing in new equipment. It would also require a longer lead time and, hence, more savings or a more secure alternative income source. You should also do some investigating to find out whether freelancing can be done successfully in your chosen field. Do companies in your field actually use freelancers? If so, how much do they pay? The answers to these questions are crucial. You might find, for example, that it is easier to make money as a freelance computer programmer than as a freelance photographer. For that matter, you may want to consider freelancing in more than one field (writing and photography, for example, or design and desktop publishing).

Whatever line of work you choose, you need to ask yourself whether you have enough skills, experience, and education or training to be able to market yourself effectively in that area. Most clients want freelancers to have at least some experience in their field or in a closely related one. They won't hire you if you're completely green. That's why it's a good idea to gain a few years of in-house experience before taking the plunge. You also want to be sure that your skills and equipment are up to date. If you can develop a specialty, such as science writing or underwater photography, so much the better. Think carefully about how much competition you're likely to encounter. If there are already large numbers of people in your area who do the same kind of work, you should try to find a way to offer something different. In such a situation a unique specialty will be even more valuable.

You also need to investigate your potential client base. Are there enough clients out there to supply you with the number of projects you'll need if you are to meet your income goals? Some fields that were formerly wide open have shrunk considerably as a result of the merger mania of recent decades. For example, the number of textbook publishers is much smaller today than it was in the 1970s, making it difficult to attract a steady flow of textbook editing projects. Under such conditions it is necessary to branch out—to do different kinds of work or seek different kinds of clients.

You can get a lot of information about freelancing in your field by simply talking to other freelancers. If you haven't already done so, this is the time to join a professional association in your chosen field. The information provided by such organizations in their newsletters and publications is invaluable, as is the networking that goes on at meetings (the latter can be a source of moral support as well). Some groups also offer job listing and referral services.

If there are national conventions or conferences in your chosen field, try to attend them. You can do a lot of networking at these events, especially in the exhibit halls. You can also get advice from your local chamber of commerce and from the Small Business Administration. They'll be listed in your phone book.

Other decisions that need to be made at the outset include the choice of a place to work and the amount and types of equipment to invest in. Ideally, you will set up an office in a spare room and buy a computer, a fax machine, and perhaps a copier, along with any other equipment required for the type of work you do (e.g., a light table if you are a photo researcher). If you already have any of these items, you're ahead of the game. If you don't, you'll need to budget accordingly. Also remember to have business cards and letterhead printed.

Above all, it's important to remember that *freelancing is a business.* You need to think of yourself as managing a small business, even if you don't have employees, inventory, or complex accounts. When you go freelance, you are going into business for yourself, and you need to ask yourself the same questions you would ask if you were launching any kind of small business.

Developing Contacts

Perhaps the most important thing you need to do before committing yourself to freelancing is to line up potential sources of work. If you are on good terms with your current employer and that employer is accustomed to hiring freelancers, you may be able to talk about your plans in advance and perhaps arrange to work on a project as soon as you go freelance. If your current job isn't too demanding, you may want to consider freelancing on the side in order to build up a client base before leaving your full-time job. In any case you should make an effort to locate potential clients before taking the plunge.

The first time I went freelance, I was expecting a baby and intended to take a few weeks off before beginning my freelance career. I mentioned my plans to my secretary, and it turned out that a friend of hers was an editor at a well-known publishing company. I called the friend, and she referred me to the managing editor of another publishing house, who asked me to take a copyediting test. I passed the test, and my résumé was placed in the file of active freelancers. A few weeks later, just when I was ready for it, I had my first copyediting job.

I can't emphasize strongly enough the importance of chasing down every possible lead in the search for clients. Call everyone you know who is even remotely connected with your field. You may be surprised at how often one of them knows someone else who may become a client or may be able to refer you to another potential client. As one successful writer advises, "Ask. Ask everyone you know—friends, family, associates. You never know who has a connection that will click for you. People want to help."[3]

It is also worthwhile to send letters and résumés to potential clients. (This will take a little research, since you need to find out the name of the appropriate person to contact.) But whether you contact clients in person, by phone, or by mail, this is not the time to be shy or modest. Focus on what clients need and how you can help them. As the writer just mentioned noted when asked how she got past the receptionist at a publishing

---

3. Judith Levy, quoted in Marcia Savin, "Ignoring *No,* Heeding *Yes,*" *The Freelancer,* November–December 1996, p. 3.

house, "I said, Give me five minutes of your time and I'll show you how I'm going to make you lots of money."[4]

Enjoy

Whatever you do, have fun. Remember that the idea behind all this is to be your own boss. With a little care and planning, you will find that freelancing is an ideal way to earn a living. You will also find that it is a very pleasant way to live. In short, you will thoroughly enjoy being your own boss.

4. Ibid.

Appendix: Some Useful Resources for Freelancers

Publications

Anderson, Sandy, *The Work at Home Balancing Act* (Avon Books).
> Offers advice and strategies to assist in determining your suitability for working at home, choosing a fitting line of work, and creating a plan for making a smooth transition.

Buff, Sheila, *Résumés for Freelancers* (Editorial Freelancers Association).
> Describes how to turn a traditional résumé into an effective marketing tool.

Editorial Freelancers Association, *Rates and Business Practices Survey.*

> Based on a survey of freelance writers, editors, and related professionals. Presents ranges of pay reported for various types of freelance work, ranging from abstracting and abridging to writing and ghostwriting.

Edwards, Paul and Sarah, *Working From Home: Everything You Need to Know About Living and Working Under the Same Roof* (G. P. Putnam's Sons).

> A comprehensive reference book for people working from home. Contains helpful information on making your home office convenient, functional, and professional; protecting your assets (legal, tax, and insurance matters); managing your home office (including "sixty-second housecleaning"); managing yourself and others; and getting business.

Freelance Editorial Association (Boston), *Code of Fair Practice,* rev. ed.

> A guide to maintaining professional relationships between freelancers and clients. Covers fees, project terms, contracts, and disputes. Includes sample agreements and invoices.

Lawler, Jennifer, *Small-Business Ownership for Creative People* (Aletheia Publications).

> Takes a step-by-step approach to starting and running the kinds of small businesses that creative people—writers, photographers, and others—are most likely to be involved in. Provides easy-to-understand business basics.

Lewis, Laurie, *What to Charge* (Aletheia Publications).

> Offers proven pricing strategies for consultants and freelancers.

Lonier, Terri, *Working Solo*

> A series of books and audio programs, along with a web site and a free newsletter, with advice for self-employed individuals, home-based business owners, consultants, and other independent professionals.

Quilter, Deborah, *The Repetitive Strain Injury Recovery Book* (Walker and Company).

> A comprehensive guide for RSI sufferers. Provides recovery and preventive tips and techniques for both home and work.

Rogers, Trumbull, *Editorial Freelancing: A Practical Guide* (Aletheia Publications).

> Presents in clear, succinct language everything the freelancer needs to know about establishing and equipping the home office, marketing editorial services, finding and keeping clients, determining and negotiating rates, billing, maintaining business records, building a basic reference library, choosing a computer and appropriate software, and setting up a retirement plan.

Rozakis, Laurie E., *The Complete Idiot's Guide to Making Money in Freelancing* (Macmillan General Reference).

> Describes, in typical "idiot guide" language, the pros and cons of full-time vs. part-time work, "idiot-proof" steps to keeping the work and the paychecks flowing in, easy techniques for managing your time and money, valuable tips for setting up your own business, and the "inside scoop" on finding and keeping clients.

Organizations

American Home Business Association
    4505 S. Wasatch Blvd., No. 140
    Salt Lake City, UT 84124
    801-273-2350

Association of Part-Time Professionals
    7700 Leesburg Pike, Ste. 216
    Falls Church, VA 22043-2615
    703-734-7975
    www.aptp.org

Editorial Freelancers Association
    71 W. 23rd St., Ste. 1910
    New York, NY 10010
    212-929-5400
    www.the-efa.org

Home Office Association of America
    909 Third Ave.
    New York, NY 10022
    800-809-4622
    www.hoaa.com

Mothers' Home Business Network
    P.O. Box 423
    East Meadow, NY 11554
    516-997-7394
    www.homeworkingmom.com

National Association for the Self-Employed
    2121 Precinct Line Rd.
    Hurst, TX 76054
    800-232-6273
    www.nase.org

National Association of Home Based Businesses
    10451 Mills Run Circle, #400
    Owing Mills, MD 21117
    410-363-3698
    www.usahomebiz.com

Small Business Administration
    409 Third St., SW
    Washington, DC 20416
    800-827-5722
    www.sba.gov/starting

Index

About the Artist

The cartoons that appear at the beginning of each chapter were drawn by artist/musician Napier Dunn. A former professional French horn player, Dunn has played in numerous orchestras, including the London Philharmonic, and has worked for newspapers and magazines throughout the world. He is currently employed as a political cartoonist with The Mercury *in Durban, South Africa, where he also practices Tai Chi, plays tennis, and is an occasional tour guide.*

About the Author

Carolyn D. Smith is a freelance editor/writer specializing in textbook development in the social sciences. Her other published works include *The Absentee American: Repatriates' Perspectives on America; Strangers at Home: Essays on the Experience of Living Overseas and Coming "Home" to a Strange Land;* and *In the Field: Readings on the Field Research Experience.* An active member of the Editorial Freelancers Association, she has served as its co-executive director and chair of its publications committee.